the saxophone handbook

A COMPLETE
GUIDE TO TONE,
TECHNIQUE,
PERFORMANCE,
& MAINTENANCE

Edited by Jonathan Feist

douglas d. skinner

This book is dedicated to my late father, Durland Skinner,
who provided saxophone lessons and insisted that I practice and study,
and to my wife Vicki, who continues to support and encourage me.

Berklee Press

Editor in Chief: Jonathan Feist
Vice President of Online Learning and Continuing Education: Debbie Cavalier
Assistant Vice President of Berklee Media: Robert F. Green
Dean of Continuing Education: Carin Nuernberg
Editorial Assistants: Dominick DiMaria, Won (Sara) Hwang, Sarah Walk
Cover Designer: Kathy Kikkert
Cover Photo: Phil Farnsworth

ISBN 978-0-87639-138-9

1140 Boylston Street
Boston, MA 02215-3693 USA
(617) 747-2146

Visit Berklee Press Online at
www.berkleepress.com

DISTRIBUTED BY

HAL•LEONARD®
CORPORATION
7777 W. BLUEMOUND RD. P.O. BOX 13819
MILWAUKEE, WISCONSIN 53213

Visit Hal Leonard Online at
www.halleonard.com

CONTENTS

CHAPTER 1

Equipment

"Poor workmen blame their tools."
—My father

Achieving saxophone excellence begins with acquiring and maintaining the proper equipment.

PURCHASING A SAXOPHONE

Selecting the right saxophone: what to do? A poor quality saxophone is a definite detriment to practicing and enjoying it. There are four basic questions to consider before purchasing a saxophone:

- How will the saxophone be used?
- Should it be a soprano, alto, tenor, or baritone?
- What are the best sources for buying saxophones?
- How should the saxophone be evaluated?

First, is the saxophone needed for beginning band, marching band, a professional ensemble, or for enthusiastic practicing at home? Perhaps, it is an upgrade from a previous model. Answers to these questions will determine how much to spend and which brand or model is suitable.

Then, will it be a soprano, alto, tenor, or baritone? The alto and tenor are the obvious choices for a first saxophone because they are common in various performance ensembles. The soprano and baritone are regarded more as specialty saxophones, and for that reason, they are usually purchased third or fourth in one's collection. Often, educational institutions have sopranos and baritones in their inventories for use in their ensembles.

For years, there were essentially three models or "lines" of saxophones available: student, intermediate, and professional. Recently, the lines of distinction have been blurred, due to the production of saxophones from Taiwan and China. The new saxophones are competing successfully with established manufacturers. Their names may not be readily identifiable, like Selmer or Yamaha, but the price tags can be considerably less. Some are of superb quality. They deserve consideration, but beware that these sources are subject to change at any time, and quality control can be an issue. Make a short list of acceptable brands and models by checking with music educators (preferably saxophonists), college saxophone instructors, or trustworthy music merchants, if you need assistance with your list.

Acquire the absolute best saxophone that your budget allows. As the price goes up, the musical and mechanical advantages improve. Consider buying a new instrument, if price is not an issue. New, shiny lacquer or plating is very appealing to some buyers. If price is a factor, consider buying an "experienced" instrument. An older model may require some repairs before it is in suitable mechanical condition, but a saxophone that is rejuvenated by a skillful technician will rival one that is "still in the plastic."

Among the professional model saxophones, there is an entirely separate category designated as "vintage"—loosely defined as any saxophone manufactured before 1970. There are legions of saxophonists devoted strictly to performing on vintage saxophones. The "vintage versus new" saxophone debate will rage on forever, and a conclusion may never be reached. It is generally accepted that vintage saxophones offer advantages and disadvantages, depending on the particular model:

Advantages	Disadvantages
unique tone quality	faulty intonation
has history	certain mouthpieces are incompatible
has personality	less durable mechanically
less depreciation	possible previous relacquering
classy engraving	more expensive (Selmer Mark VI e.g.)

The following "selection tree" illustrates possible choices among student, intermediate, and professional saxophones. Each category includes vintage saxophones.

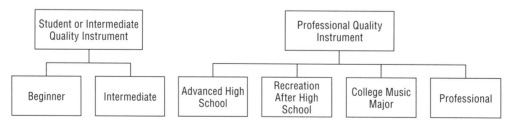

Fig. 1.1. Saxophone Selection Tree

The good news is that new and used saxophones are readily available. There are many reputable national instrument companies that maintain large inventories of new and used saxophones and may sell them at reduced prices. An Internet search will quickly reveal multiple sources and provide price comparisons. Local music merchants may not keep very large collections, but they can often provide timely repairs and are accessible for any issues regarding a saxophone purchased from them. Also, check newspaper listings, eBay, and pawnshops, but "buyer beware." Such instruments do not carry a warranty and may have been abused. In pawnshops, there is the possibility that you might even purchase a stolen instrument! Another option is renting. Many stores apply the rental price to the sale price. Usually, there is an interest charge added, so that over time, the overall cost is higher. "Renting to buy" is still a viable option, though, if there is a possibility that ownership will be short-term.

When it's time to make a decision on a particular saxophone, it is also time for a trial test and evaluation to diagnose its mechanical condition and intonation tendencies. Saxophones of a particular brand may look alike but may differ greatly in quality. Regard each saxophone as unique, possessing its own inherent assets and deficiencies.

If you are a beginner, enlist the assistance of a trusted evaluator. This person can be a band teacher, private lesson instructor, or a more experienced player. Also, if possible, a saxophone repair specialist should have the opportunity to examine any used saxophone before payment is made.

Take a mouthpiece, ligature, and reeds to the test site. Bringing cork grease is also advisable. An electronic tuner is absolutely required!

Music stores usually service their instruments before a sale and often allow customers to keep the instruments for a few days before making a final decision. Private owners sometimes offer the same opportunity, but it may have to be negotiated. Have a repair technician check for leaks, critical dents, spring tension, and pad condition. Make a musical evaluation as well. Play the saxophone, and check every pitch for intonation accuracy with the tuner. Use the intonation chart provided on figure 3.11. All saxophones have slightly faulty intonation tendencies on particular notes (see the section on intonation, chapter 3). However, if the tuner indicates a pitch variation of 15 cents or more, this is severe and problematic. The intonation/trial test should be performed by a proficient saxophonist. Less experienced saxophonists may not have a stable embouchure formation or breath support, and the test results may be misleading.

Saxophones are available in a variety of finishes: lacquer (most common), black nickel, bare brass, silver plate, gold plate, and in combinations. The different finishes alter the tone quality marginally, if at all. This debate continues. A relacquered saxophone is a red flag. To remove the old lacquer, the saxophone may have been buffed, which also may have removed metal, thus weakening its structure. Signs of relacquering on an experienced saxophone include indistinct engraving, a bright or brassy color, or a blurred serial number.

To summarize, there are numerous varieties of saxophones available, and the industry is constantly changing. Base your selection on price and recommendations of knowledgeable saxophonists, especially when scouting inexpensive instruments. Among professional quality saxophones, certain "giants" have stood the test of time and reign supreme, whether it is their current or vintage product. Choosing a saxophone should be an entirely personal choice based on input from colleagues, play-testing, and research. Simple but thorough procedures will help you find that "perfect" saxophone.

MOUTHPIECES

The mouthpiece may be the least understood piece of saxophone equipment by the novice. Knowledge is crucial, however, because the mouthpiece is the connection from the player to the instrument. To complicate matters, a jazz mouthpiece *and* a classical mouthpiece may be necessary, because tonal and stylistic requirements for those performance mediums are so different. Achieving a desirable tone for a particular performing venue is greatly dependent upon mouthpiece selection.

When we listen to a saxophone's tone, we describe it with adjectives like "dark" or "bright," "thin" or "thick," "raucous" or "fluid," etc. It is possible to change tone quality from one extreme to another, or anywhere in between, simply by changing mouthpieces.

One misconception is that the mouthpiece material determines the timbre of the tone. The composition of a mouthpiece can be metal, hard rubber, plastic, wood, ceramic, or other compounds. A natural assumption is that metal is louder, more penetrating, and thus suitable for jazz, while hard rubber is more suitable for classical playing. However, it is not the metal itself that is responsible for producing a jazz tone. Marcel Mule, the legendary classical saxophonist of the Paris Conservatory (and many of his students) used a Selmer metal C star mouthpiece for years. The tone he produced was clearly of a symphonic nature. Tone quality is much more affected by mouthpiece chamber and facing design. Material ranks a distant third.

The jazz performer may require quite a different mouthpiece. In order to compete with eight to ten brass players and an amplified rhythm section, the mouthpiece must be capable of generating maximum power. A jazz mouthpiece may require a wider tip opening and a smaller chamber for increased projection, or perhaps a raised baffle. Like the classical versions, the choices are numerous and can be perplexing. Consult available manufacturer mouthpiece comparison charts to get an overview, and talk to as many experienced jazz saxophonists and teachers as you can. Keep in mind that wider tip openings require softer reeds for ease of emission. If at all possible, try the mouthpiece before buying it.

The various components of a mouthpiece:

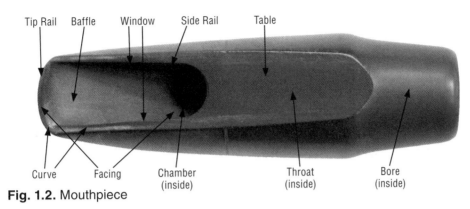

Fig. 1.2. Mouthpiece

Tip Opening

The *tip opening* is the distance measured between the tip rail of the mouthpiece and the tip of the reed. Generally, wider or open-tip openings require a softer reed as compensation. Jazz musicians typically favor a wide tip opening/soft reed combination, while classical musicians usually opt for a closer tip opening/harder reed to produce the desired timbre. These are merely generalizations, however. Adding to the confusion, mouthpiece manufacturers have varying systems of indicating tip opening measurements. Some use numbers such as #4 or #5, with #5 being more open. Some add a "star" to the numbers such as #4, #4*. The star is usually a tip opening between two numbers such as 4 and 5. One manufacturer's #5 may not equate to another's, which further complicates comparing tip openings. Some mouthpiece manufacturers refer to tip openings in millimeters, such as .072. Obviously, with so many different manufacturers and measuring systems, it can be bewildering. Fortunately, some major musical instrument companies have handy reference charts online or in their catalogs to facilitate comparisons. It is advisable to examine these mouthpiece charts for a clear understanding of the differences.

Facing

The *facing* describes the distance from the flat portion of the side rails to the tip rail. It includes the curve. Facings can be long (which favors the low register), medium, or short (which favors the upper register).

Curve

The *curve* is crucial to a mouthpiece. As mentioned, the facing is one of two prominent factors that define a mouthpiece's playing characteristics. The curve begins at the "break-point," where the reed and mouthpiece separate, and continues to the tip rail.

The curve can be a short or long measurement and is usually designated as such by the mouthpiece manufacturer. Many manufacturers produce only one type of curve. Similar to the facing, a long curve favors the low register and requires a stiffer reed. The short curve does the opposite.

Table

The *table* is the flat area below the facing. It may not be safe to assume that a table is flat, even on a new mouthpiece. Subjecting a mouthpiece to intense heat can warp the surface. No reed will vibrate properly after that. It is advisable to have the table checked by a mouthpiece expert, especially after years of use.

Window

The *window* is the open area where the player's breath enters the mouthpiece. The length of the window should approximately match the length of the reed vamp (see the section on reeds, page 9).

Baffle

Just below the tip, inside the window, is the *baffle*. The baffle has tremendous influence on tone color. A raised (convex) baffle compresses the air stream, resulting in a brighter tone with more edge. Jazz players seek a mouthpiece with a raised baffle. A low baffle (concave) produces a darker timbre with less edge, which is more suitable for concert literature.

A popular practice for many years among saxophonists seeking a louder, brighter tone is to place a "wedge" on top of the existing baffle. Wedges can be made from any material that will stick to the mouthpiece surface. Plexiglass is a popular choice because it can be filed to the desired shape and thickness. Wedges can also be composed of wax, epoxy, or other substances. Once inserted on top of the baffle, a classical style mouthpiece instantly becomes a "screamer," impersonating a jazz mouthpiece. The closer the wedge is to the tip, the more volume and edge is produced. Beware of the consequences, however. It is likely that the high notes will be excruciatingly sharp with a high baffle. Any old wedge will not do. It must conform to the overall mouthpiece design for good intonation. A properly designed jazz mouthpiece will contain a high baffle or built-in wedge. Keep in mind, however, that the manufacturers experimented and tested the design for a long time before finalizing it.

Tip Rail

At the end of the window, at the mouthpiece tip, is a carefully finished and precise *tip rail*. The thickness of the tip rail impacts response and tone color to a great degree. It is essential that the tip rail be a smooth surface, free of nicks and dents.

Side Rails

The *side rails* outline the window and serve as a vibrating surface for the reed. Inspect the rails closely for nicks, scratches, or dents. The two rails should also be the same width. Side rails must be maintained in pristine condition to facilitate good tone production and response. Small imperfections in the side rails may or may not affect the playability of a mouthpiece. If the damage is significant, replace the mouthpiece or have it "refaced" by a competent mouthpiece technician.

Chamber

The *chamber* is the interior of the mouthpiece that extends to the bore where the mouthpiece attaches to the saxophone neck. Timbre is influenced by the chamber more than any other part of the mouthpiece. Chamber designs range from large to small, from round side walls to straight, and from single to double chambers. As a general guideline, smaller chambers produce brighter tones than larger chambers. Thus, as expected, jazz mouthpieces usually have a smaller bore design and classical mouthpieces a larger one. A comparison can be made with brass mouthpieces. Symphony brass players use a large cup (chamber) mouthpiece, whereas brass players in big bands often use a smaller cup.

Many mouthpieces on the market today are manufactured in one chamber size only. For example, the popular Selmer CS 80 mouthpiece has one chamber size but has several tip openings: C star, D, E, etc. A few, like Meyer and Berg Larsen, have multiple chamber sizes. Meyer mouthpieces have small, medium, and large chambers. Berg Larsen mouthpieces are designed with four different baffle heights: 0 (brightest), 1, 2, and 3.

Throat

Between the chamber and the bore is the *throat*, which is most often a round, half-round, or square shape. Each shape influences tone production to some degree.

Bore

Essentially, the *bore* is a continuation of the saxophone neck. The connection should be snug for optimum response. Do not allow a loose fit. Saxophonists with both a jazz mouthpiece and a classical mouthpiece may discover that the thickness of the cork on the neck may not be suitable for both. Wrapping the cork with paper is a temporary fix. It is possible to "swell" the cork by coating it with Vaseline or cork grease and rotating the neck slowly above heat from a stove. It is also possible to burn the cork right off the neck if it gets too close to the heat! An excellent temporary substitute is plumber's Teflon tape, wrapped securely around the old cork. The tape can be coated with cork grease.

Measuring a Mouthpiece

Understanding the design and function of mouthpieces is the first step in the selection process. With some certainty, expect uniformity and precision in the bore, baffle, and chamber dimensions. Because of the importance of the facing, saxophonists should check these measurements personally. There are many suspicious mouthpieces that warrant a closer inspection with precision measuring tools, because their side rails aren't the same or the curve is too long or short. Many mouthpieces are ruined by amateurs attempting to reface them, but even some new mouthpieces fail this kind of inspection. In my experience, one out of three mouthpieces has incorrect measurements.

Over fifty years ago, Erick Brand was a foreman in the woodwind division of Selmer. He devised a mouthpiece measuring kit consisting of a set of feeler gauges of various thicknesses to measure the curve of the side rails and a tool to measure the tip opening. Some of those kits are still around, but now there are newer versions available.

Measuring kits will likely include a glass gauge for measuring the side rails and a tip gauge to measure the tip opening. Feeler gauges will probably be included, as well. If not, obtain a set of feeler gauges used to measure spark plug gaps from an automotive store. The feeler gauges needed for an alto saxophone are .0015, .010, .024, .034, and .050. If you anticipate measuring soprano, tenor, and baritone saxophone mouthpieces and clarinet and bass clarinet mouthpieces, you can invest in additional feeler gauges .017, .026, .037, .063, .078, .093, .109, and .125. Take them apart so that they can be used interchangeably.

Insert the gauges, one at a time, thinnest to thickest, between the side rails and the glass gauge. Slide the gauges down the side rails until the resistance stops them. Take readings of half-millimeters, on both sides, and write the numbers down. Follow the same procedure with each gauge. At this point, there are five written numbers in two columns.

	Left Side	Right Side
.0015		
.010		
.024		
.034		
.050		

If one side is different from the other, measure again to be sure. If the result is the same, the mouthpiece has mismatched side rails and should be refaced or replaced. If the kit does not include a tip gauge, stack the feeler gauges and insert them at the tip rail. This reveals an approximate tip-opening measurement. [1]

[1] From Dan Torosian, mouthpiece technician in Austin, Texas

The Incredible Lemon Treatment

Over time, the table and side rails accumulate a film, despite frequent washings. The film is there but may not be visible, and it can degrade the mouthpiece's performance. To remove it, take a fresh lemon, and slice off a piece large enough to grip the skin. Scrub the mouthpiece table and side rails with the inside of the lemon. The acidic nature of the lemon juice removes the film. Place a sheet of white paper on a flat surface, and polish the table and side rails. Wash and dry the mouthpiece, and try it. On some mouthpieces, this may not make a difference. On others, the change in sound and response is incredible! [2]

Final Thoughts on Mouthpieces

Every saxophonist has a tone that is unique, like a fingerprint or voiceprint. The search and discovery for that unique tone involves a certain amount of mouthpiece experimentation. With each change of mouthpiece, however, the search can become more and more disorienting.

There are plenty of "mouthpieceaholics" who spend their lives devoted to an endless search with no conclusion. Experimentation is fine, but set limits. Within a category of mouthpieces designed for a particular venue (say, concert music), the differences are subtle. Settle on one or two, and stick with them.

SELECTING AND ADJUSTING REEDS

There is a time in a saxophonist's development when the quality of a reed should begin to play a more prominent role. To truly achieve a high degree of artistry requires devoting the time and patience necessary to learn reed adjustment techniques. Double-reed players understand this necessity. Single-reed players should follow their lead. The chart below represents a condensed version of many years of experimentation with reed adjustment. It should be stressed that only a few minutes a week are required for you to maintain four performance-ready reeds. There are significant differences between reeds that are balanced and adjusted and those that are not.

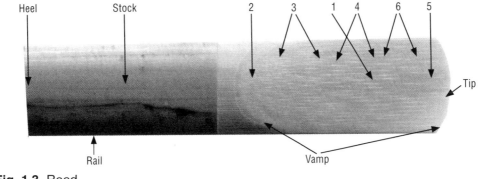

Fig. 1.3. Reed

[2] From Peter Deley, mouthpiece technician in Portland, Oregon

Objective: to have four performance-ready reeds, rotated daily

Tools

- #600 (extra fine) sandpaper
- piece of glass or plexiglass slightly larger than the reed
- reed trimmer
- reed holder/protector
- reed knife or scraper

Glue a piece of the sandpaper to one side of the glass, using rubber cement. When the sandpaper is unusable, simply peel it off and replace it, using the rubber cement again. Place the reed on the other side of the glass for adjustments with the reed knife. The piece of glass can stay in the saxophone case, available for use at any location.

Fig 1.4. PerfectaReed Reed Measuring/Balancing Device

Consider purchasing the PerfectaReed, a handy and highly accurate device for measuring a reed's balance. It is quite rare for a mass-manufactured reed to have the same thickness measurements on the left and right sides. Simply insert the reed with the left side against the bar, and position it on stations 1 to 8, writing down the thickness in millimeters. Reverse the reed, and measure the right side the same way. Compare the two columns and scrape the heavier side, to better balance the reed. Tone projection and resistance improve dramatically.

Purchasing Reeds

Buy unopened boxes of reeds with a strength suited to the mouthpiece.

Conditioning Process

Conditioning and adjusting a reed requires a few minutes a day for four consecutive days.

Day 1

Wet the heel end first, then place it tip-side down in a glass of water to soak for 10 minutes. Play for 5 minutes in the middle register. Let it dry overnight.

Day 2

Repeat the first day process.

Day 3

Sand the flat side with the sandpaper flat on a table. Be sure to avoid sanding the tip by keeping it off the sandpaper. Soak it for 10 minutes, and play in all registers for 5 minutes.

Day 4

Sand the flat side. Soak it for 10 minutes, play in all registers, and make adjustments with the knife or scraper.

Reed Adjustments: Simple Is Best

After completing the conditioning process, the reeds may have more/less resistance or a change in tone quality. The final step is to make adjustments to improve those aspects of the reed. After numerous years of experimenting, I have found that only three adjustments are usually necessary. Refer to the reed chart for adjustments.

A good reed candidate is one that has a full high register but is resistant: too hard. If the high register is weak, try using the reed clipper, or store the reed in a box to try a year or two later. Perhaps it will work well on another mouthpiece.

- Step 1. Shave areas 2 and 3 on both sides of the vamp, equal amounts. This improves the low notes, and often, it is all that needs to be done.
- Step 2. Shave areas 4 and 6 on both sides.
- Step 3. As a last resort after completing steps 1 and 2, if the reed is still too resistant, gently scrape the entire vamp, going towards the tip. To some, this area, which includes the "heart," is off limits entirely. Don't believe it! A careful scraping in this area can make all the difference and does not destroy the reed's balance, unless overdone.

Avoid shaving area 5, the tip. The reed is already thin enough there, and you stand a good chance of destroying it completely.

Daily Care

Each day of use, sand the flat side on sandpaper (avoiding the tip), and soak for 10 minutes in water before playing. After six weeks of use, try soaking the reed in a solution of 75 percent hydrogen peroxide and 25 percent water. Then, scrub it lightly with a toothbrush. Sometimes, the hydrogen peroxide will revive a worn-out reed.

Advice for Scraping Reeds

Scrape lightly with the knife, a little at a time. Reed shavings should appear as fine particles, not small chunks of cane. Limit reed working to short sessions, and be patient!

Once you have four reeds that are performance-ready, it is a good idea to begin the conditioning process on two or three new ones. Soon, they will be needed to move into the rotation, to replace ones that have deteriorated. Of course, not every reed will become suitable for a performance, but they might be useable for practicing.

Never just throw a reed away. Store rejected reeds in a container, and try them again in a year or two. Some of those stored reeds may prove to be of value later.

Reed cane grows in the south of France, the Var region. The climate is sufficiently humid and conducive to growing, cultivating, and manufacturing the best cane. For a commercial reed to perform at its best, it is important to provide a similar environment, once purchased. In areas of the world where humidity is too low, it can be advantageous to artificially create the proper environment by building a reed box humidifier.

This inexpensive homemade reed box will store reeds in approximately 72 percent humidity.

Reed Box Humidifier

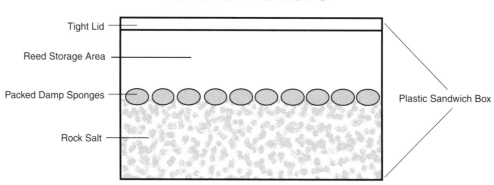

Fig. 1.5. Reed Box Humidifier

LIGATURES

What good is a vibrant, responsive reed that is stifled by a poorly designed or ill-fitting ligature? Example: A not-so-well known saxophonist used a metal automobile hose clamp for a ligature. Every time the saxophonist assembled the reed and mouthpiece, he pulled out a screwdriver to tighten his "ligature." The reeds vibrated, but most assuredly, not as well as they could have. Notice the large inventory of ligatures advertised, each touting a revolutionary and unique design.

Essentially, a ligature should hold a reed in place without constricting its vibrations. There is a difference in response and tone quality among ligatures, so experimenting with them is a good idea. Like mouthpieces, however, find one and stick with it.

Ligatures generally are either fabric or metal and are classified as "standard" and "ultra." A *standard* ligature is generally inexpensive and may have one or two screws to secure it to the reed and mouthpiece. *Ultra* ligatures come in a variety of designs and make contact with the reed in varying ways.

Some manufacturers have combined the two types successfully—for example, a fabric body with a metal surface that contacts the reed. Some saxophonists insist that there is no audible difference in tone quality among ligatures. Others argue that there is a sizeable difference.

Some descriptions pertaining to ligatures and tone include:

- bright/dark tone
- edgy/stuffy tone
- more center/less center
- free blowing/resistant response
- faster/slower articulation

Ease of use, mouthpiece fit, visual appeal, and especially performance are the major factors to consider, when searching for the right ligature. A university clarinet professor I know has used a black, 27-inch shoelace as a ligature for over forty years. He found that the shoelace satisfied his definition of a good ligature: providing even distribution of pressure across the stock of the reed. The shoestring is similar to the old string ligatures used by German clarinet players many years ago. The 27-inch shoestring is certainly an economical choice!

NECK STRAPS

There are two important requirements of a neck strap: it should be comfortable and secure. Although neck straps are comparatively inexpensive accessories, a good fit and reliability are of paramount importance. In recent years, new designs that incorporate shoulder straps and harnesses have alleviated neck strain by distributing the saxophone's weight on the shoulders instead of the neck. For baritone saxophonists, these are a blessing. Materials for neck straps include beaded chain, heavy string, cord, neoprene, or nylon. The hook can be plastic, metal, a swivel hook, or an open hook. Whatever style and design is preferred, it must be quickly adjustable, comfortable, dependable, and promote good posture. Periodically, check the strap, and especially the hook, for excessive wear. A strap that suddenly breaks produces disastrous results.

THE WELL-EQUIPPED SAXOPHONIST

A tuner and a metronome should be standard equipment for any serious musician. For practicing and teaching, they are indispensable.

The well-equipped saxophonist possesses and uses the following items:

- metronome
- tuner
- surplus of new reeds
- reed equipment
- basic repair tools
- digital recorder

A digital recorder will revolutionize practicing, rehearsals, or teaching. This palm-sized device can record several hours of a practice session, lesson, or rehearsal, producing a file that can be downloaded to a computer via a USB cable and converted to an MP3 file. The file can be e-mailed or recorded to a CD. The quality of sound is astonishing. The digital recorder is a "must have" for the well-equipped saxophonist.

CHAPTER 2

Repairing Saxophones

The importance of maintaining and repairing a saxophone is obvious. It is impossible to perform or practice efficiently if the instrument has leaking pads or sluggish key action.

These procedures can be done at home. Begin with general maintenance, then contact a repair supply company for supplies and tools. Continue progressing to more advanced procedures as you acquire skills. Soldering and dent removal work should be done in a competent repair shop. Space and more expensive equipment are required for those types of repairs.

BASIC MAINTENANCE CHECKLIST

This checklist/timetable requires a minimum amount of effort and pays big dividends. With regularly scheduled maintenance, a saxophone will remain in excellent condition.

Daily (After Practicing)

- Remove the mouthpiece from the neck.
- Remove the reed from the mouthpiece, and place it in a protective reed holder.
- Protect the mouthpiece with a ligature and cap.
- Wipe the saxophone and mouthpiece with a soft cloth.

Weekly

- Wash the mouthpiece in lukewarm, soapy water. Scrub lightly with a soft brush.
- Wash the neck as you did the mouthpiece, but covering the octave keypad with aluminum foil.
- Inspect the condition of pads.
- Confirm that all screws and rods are flush with the posts.

Monthly

- Clean the accumulated dust around keys and springs with a pipe cleaner or small brush.
- Remove any discoloration on the mouthpiece with a brush and toothpaste.

Yearly

- Dip a pipe cleaner in a 50/50 solution of denatured alcohol and neatsfoot oil. Coat each pad and let dry outside the case for 24 hours.
- Loosen pivot screws and rods one full turn, and oil them with a high quality oil. Tighten the screws, but not excessively.
- Apply the lemon treatment to the mouthpiece (see page 9).

Denatured alcohol and neatsfoot oil are found in hardware stores. Keeping the mixture stirred, lightly coat each pad. The alcohol cleans grit and grime from the pads while the oil soaks in and softens the leather. Perform this procedure annually if the pads are old or in a dried condition. If the pads are still soft and flexible, do not apply the mixture. The pads can become so soft that the tone-hole rims may cut through the skin of the pads.

To cure sticking pads, take a piece of very fine sandpaper (such as #600), place the grit side down on the tone hole, depress the key using light pressure, and pull the paper out. This cleans the tone hole rims. Then, coat the pads with lemon oil (furniture oil) applied with a pipe cleaner. Repeat the procedure if necessary.

REPAIRS

The ability to make emergency repairs on an ailing saxophone provides a feeling of security. The first step is to make a thorough mechanical evaluation of the saxophone before undertaking any of the repair procedures.

At some point, despite following a program of routine maintenance, more serious mechanical problems may develop. How much will it cost, and how long will the saxophone be in the shop? Perhaps, it is time to learn simple repair procedures. A tool investment of $200 to $300 is all that is necessary to get under way.

Repair supplies are available from suppliers such as Ferree's in Battle Creek, Michigan, or MusicMedic.com and others. Besides selling repair tools, they also offer instruction and advice.

Building a Personal Repair Kit

The following tools and supplies can be obtained from instrument repair supply sources, local hardware stores, or in the home. Store them in a portable container such as a fishing tackle box. A personal toolkit should include:

key oil	needle
Weldwood Contact Cement (small bottle)	6-inch ruler
small scissors	small files
needle nose pliers	smooth jaw, flat nose pliers
spring hook	serrated jaw, flat nose pliers
tweezers	denatured alcohol
small screwdriver set	channel lock pliers
1/16-inch sheet cork	jeweler's anvil
1/8-inch sheet cork	assortment of needle springs
3/32-inch sheet cork	alcohol lamp or micro torch
single-edge razor blades	metal hammer
medium grit sandpaper	wire cutters
replacement pads	key leveling wedges
stick shellac	leak light

TROUBLESHOOTING

Able to get a tone, but not specific pitches:
- open or bent key that is supposed to be closed
- bent rod or unscrewed rod that prevents a closed key from seating
- something lodged in the bore of the instrument

Will not play index finger's B-flat:
- adjustment screw on bridge B-flat lever adjusted incorrectly, not closing the "bis" key

Produces a "crow" sound (upper and lower octaves sound at the same time):
- clogged octave tube (there are two), one on the neck and one on the upper portion of the instrument

Will not play lower octave:
- bent octave key mechanism; octave key pad should be open on high A, closed on G

Warbling sound in low register:
- missing cork or poor adjustment in left little finger key cluster
- mouthpiece may not be far enough on the cork
- neck cork and mouthpiece not a snug fit
- leaks in the lower pads

Excessive clatter in keys:
- missing or worn corks or felts

Keys not opening or closing:

- weak spring tension
- rod is binding at post
- pivot screw on a long rod is too tight

The following repair procedures are listed progressively, from easy to difficult.

KEY CORKING

Cork acts as a buffer between two pieces of metal, silencing the action. It also affects key height and regulates closing of some pads. Synthetic material such as Teflon material may also be used in this procedure.

Tools/Materials

- 1/8-inch sheet cork
- 1/16-inch sheet cork
- Weldwood Contact Cement (in a jar with brush applicator, not a tube)
- single-edge razor blade
- medium-grit sandpaper strip or small file
- sewing needle or saxophone needle spring

Fig. 2.1. Materials for Key Corking

Repair Procedure

This procedure can be accomplished with the key on or off the saxophone, depending on the key's location.

1. Completely remove the old cork and any glue.
2. Cut a piece of cork the correct length and width with the razor blade.
3. Spear the cork piece with a needle.
4. Spread a thin layer of contact cement both on the cork and on the metal surface.
5. Wait. Contact cement requires at least 12 minutes to "set up" before it is ready for use.
6. When the cement is ready, attach the cork to the metal using the needle, avoiding contact with the cement.
7. Press the key lightly to hold in place.
   - If the cork is too thick, sand or file the cork to the desired thickness.
   - If the key was removed from the saxophone, replace it.

Sometimes, the sanding can be done with the key on the saxophone, but it may be necessary to remove it again.

Fig. 2.2. Key Corking

CORKING THE NECK

Tools/Materials

- 1/16-inch sheet cork
- contact cement
- ruler
- pencil
- file or sandpaper
- single-edge razor blade
- smooth jaw, flat-nose pliers
- denatured alcohol

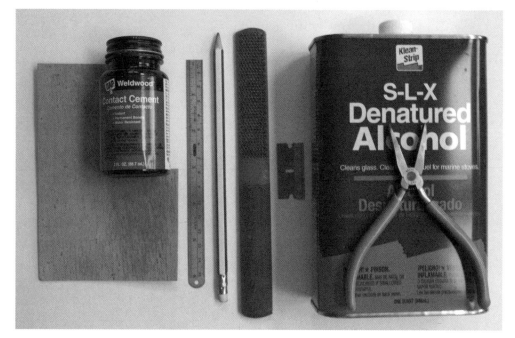

Fig. 2.3. Repairing Materials

Repair Procedure

1. Scrape off the old cork completely.
2. Lightly sand the metal surface with #600 (extra fine) sandpaper, avoiding any lacquered portion.
3. Clean with denatured alcohol and a rag.
4. Measure the cork for correct width with a ruler, and draw a line on the cork indicating the length and width required. When calculating the length, remember that one end must overlap the other end by a quarter inch.
5. Score the cork lines (about halfway through) with the razor blade, and break the piece off cleanly.

Fig. 2.4. Quarter-Inch Cork

6. With the pliers, squeeze the entire cork surface, which will make it more flexible.
7. Measure back one quarter-inch from one end, and file a taper to the tip.

Fig. 2.5. Tapered Cork

8. Spread a thin layer of contact cement on top of the tapered edge, on the bottom flat side of the cork and on the neck. Allow the cement to dry for 12 to 15 minutes.
9. Place the tapered edge (facing up) on the end of the neck, and press with both thumbs firmly to adhere the cork to the metal.
10. Continue working the cork around the neck surface slowly, keeping it aligned, pressing firmly with the thumbs. There should be no gaps between the cork and neck.

Fig. 2.6. Cork Wrapped Around Neck

11. Overlap the cork, past the tapered edge, and cut the excess cork off with the razor blade.
12. File or sand the cork *with* the grain, constantly rotating the neck clockwise.
13. Blend in the cork with the end of the neck until flush.
14. Apply cork grease, and test frequently until the mouthpiece slides on comfortably.

Do not force the mouthpiece, as this could tear the cork, and the entire procedure would have to be repeated.

NECK AND BODY ADJUSTMENT

Tools/Materials

- channel-lock pliers
- masking tape

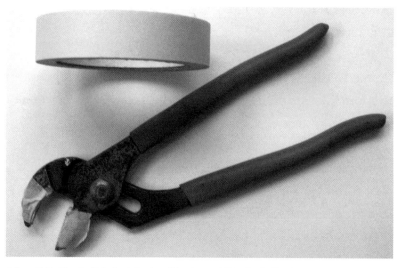

Fig. 2.7. Tools/Materials for Neck and Body Adjustment

Repair Procedure

Occasionally, the neck becomes so loose that it cannot be secured with the tightening screw.

1. Remove the screw and the neck. Cover the teeth of the channel-lock pliers and the receiver with masking tape or cloth to avoid scratching the metal.
2. *Gently* squeeze the two halves of the receiver together, with the pliers, directly on the area where the screw was removed. Too much pressure with the pliers will make it impossible to insert the neck.
3. Insert the tightening screw.

If the neck will not insert in the receiver, a special tool is needed to enlarge the receiver—a job for a repair technician.

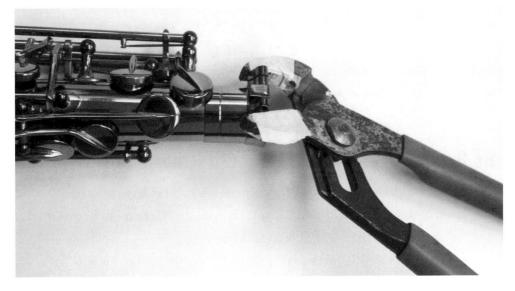

Fig. 2.8. Tightening the Neck with Taped Channel-Lock Pliers

MECHANISM ADJUSTMENTS

Tools/Materials

- cork of different thicknesses or sheet Teflon, tech cork, etc.
- screwdriver
- spring hook

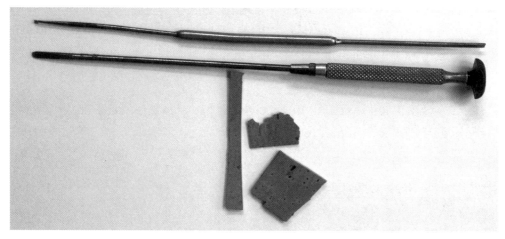

Fig. 2.9. Tools/Materials for Mechanism Adjustment

Repair Procedure: Bis B-Flat Adjustment Screw

Even if no leak light is available, this procedure can be accomplished.

1. Just above the right hand F key, there is an adjustment screw on most saxophones that regulates the Bis key lever.
   - If the screw is turned too far clockwise, the low notes will not sound, because the right hand pads will not close.
   - If it is turned too far counterclockwise, the B-flat fingering using the two index fingers will not sound.
   - To adjust, turn the screw counterclockwise until the B-flat doesn't sound, and then turn it clockwise until it does.
2. Make sure that the right-hand stack pads also close.

This adjustment screw is now set reasonably correctly.

- A leak light is preferred for the most accurate adjustment.
- Some older model saxophones may not have this adjustment screw, and leaks must be addressed by adding or subtracting cork.

Repair Procedure: G-Sharp Adjustment Screw

Located directly above the G-sharp keypad is an adjustment screw designed to keep the G-sharp keypad closed when the right-hand keys are pressed. Vibrations can cause adjustment screws to turn by themselves.

- If the screw is turned too far counterclockwise, the G-sharp keypad will remain open.

- If the screw is turned too far clockwise, it will prevent the right-hand keypads from closing. Low B and B-flat notes will not sound without a lot of effort.
- Adjust the screw counterclockwise, then clockwise, in small increments until the low B and B-flat respond.
- Like all adjustment screws, a thin coat of clear fingernail polish will hold them in place, yet the seal can be broken with a twist of a screwdriver.

Repair Procedure: Octave Key Adjustment

The octave keypad on the top of the neck is designed to be open from high A and up, closed on G sharp and below.

- Often, the tubing material that covers the lever that contacts the neck ring is missing. Replace it with heat-shrink tubing or electrician's tape.
- If the octave keypad stays open when fingering a G (with octave key), hold the pad closed with the palm of the hand, and gently push the ring outward with the thumb.
- If the octave keypad stays closed on G, bend the ring inward.

BINDING KEYS OR RODS

Keys should move freely in an upward and downward manner with no hesitation or friction.

- If a key is binding, the first procedure is to loosen the pivot screw or long rod about a quarter turn. Often, this will immediately free the action.
- If not, either the rod or the key tubing is bent or rusted.
- Remove the key and screw/rod.

To test for a bent rod, roll it on a table. Any bend will be noticeable by the way it rolls.

- Straightening a long rod should be done in a repair shop.
- Once it is straight again, oil the rod, place it inside the key, and flip the key end-over-end. It should swing freely like a gymnast on a high bar, with no binding.

ADJUSTING OR REPLACING NEEDLE SPRINGS

Tools/Materials

- serrated jaw, thin, long-nose pliers
- flat metal surface (like a jeweler's anvil)
- assortment of needle springs
- alcohol lamp or micro torch
- spring hook
- metal hammer
- wire cutters

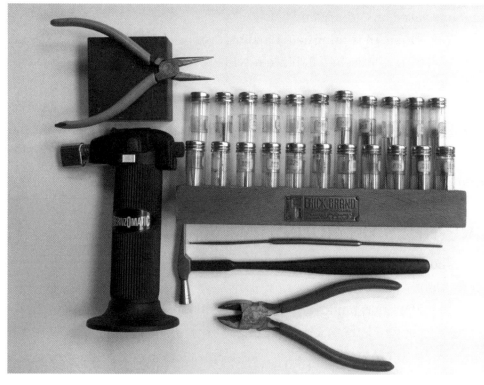

Fig. 2.10. Tools/Materials for Adjusting or Replacing Needle Springs

Repair Procedure

1. Remove the keys to get to the particular spring.
2. To add tension to a spring, place the pliers on the spring, touching the post with the sides of the pliers. Bend the spring in the opposite direction of where the spring engages the key (see figure 2.11).

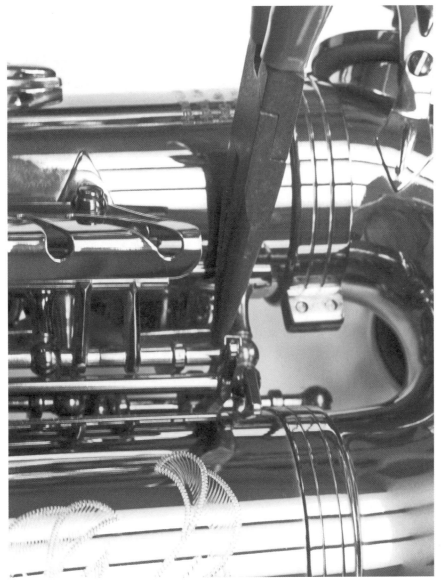

Fig. 2.11. Adjusting the Needle Spring

3. To remove the spring, cut it with the wire cutters almost flush with the post, leaving a nub protruding.

4. Place one jaw of the pliers on the nub and the other (covered with masking tape) on the post.

5. Gently squeeze the spring out the back of the post, and pull it out with the pliers. The spring only goes in and out of the post in one direction.

6. Select a spring of the same length and thickness as the old one. If the spring is too long, cut to length with the wire cutters. It should pass through the post snugly.

7. If using blue steel springs, heat the flared end of the spring over the alcohol lamp until it is very hot. Be sure to use denatured alcohol in the lamp.

8. Place the heated end on the jeweler's anvil or flat metal surface and hammer it until the end is flared. Some stainless steel springs already have flared ends so this step is not necessary.

9. Push the pointed end through the post. Pull it until the flared end catches in the post.

10. Place one blade of the pliers on the post and the other on the end of the spring. Squeeze until the flared end is flush with the post.

11. Create tension (see Step 2) on the spring.

12. Replace the key, and push the pointed end into the notch on the key with the spring hook.

PAD REPLACEMENT

Tools/Materials

- replacement pad
- leak light
- set of key leveling wedges
- stick shellac
- spring hook
- screwdriver
- needle
- alcohol lamp or micro torch
- smooth jaw needle-nose pliers

Fig. 2.12. Tools/Materials for Pad Replacement

Repair Procedure

There are two basic techniques for replacing and seating a saxophone pad. One method is to remedy leaks by adding *shims*—thin pieces of material glued on the back of the pad at leak locations. This method assumes that the keys and tone hole rims are already level. Another way, as described below, is to remove leaks by *slightly* bending the key cup. This method works very well and is quick.

1. Remove the key, and scrape out the old pad and shellac.
2. Test the size of the replacement pad by placing it in the key cup. It should fit easily, with no bunching at the sides.
3. Heat the outside of the key cup (without the pad inserted) until you can smear a thin layer of stick shellac over the entire key cup surface. You may have to hold the key with pliers because the metal warms up quickly.
4. Before the shellac hardens, place the new pad into the key cup and tap it down until it is level.
5. Mark the top/center point as "12:00" with a Magic Marker. This mark insures that if the pad is removed it will be put back in at the same position.
6. Assemble the key back on the saxophone, and hook the spring in place.
7. Insert the leak light into the bore opposite the new pad.
8. Slowly close the pad until there is a small "ring of light" between the pad and the rim (figure 2.13). The "ring" should appear even all the way around. If one side of the pad is closer to the rim than the other, the pad will leak. Be sure to close the pad with *normal* finger pressure. Do not squeeze it shut.

 Ring of Light

Fig. 2.13. Ring of Light

9. For a large leak (approximately one quarter of the pad or more), glue a thin paper shim underneath the pad where it leaks, using contact cement.
   a. Test again with the leak light.
   b. When the pad closes evenly, remove the pad once again.
   c. Follow steps 3 to 8 listed above.
   d. Clean the rim of the tone hole on the saxophone to remove any excess.
10. *If there is a small leak* (at 8:00, for example), place a thin key-leveling wedge on the opposite side, which is closing too soon.
    a. Using *gentle* thumb pressure, push directly on the leaking side of the cup (figure 2.14).
    b. Check with the light again. The leak could be smaller, gone, or now it may be leaking on the other side.

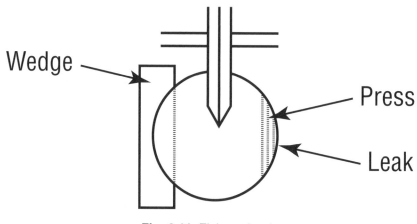

Fig. 2.14. Fixing a Leak

This is a trial-and-error process that improves with practice. Just remember not to push too hard. Just "nudge." It is not uncommon to repair several leaks in different locations before the pad finally seats.

1. If the leak is very small, place a needle under the pad, and gently lift the pad upward from the cup.

2. Check with the leak light again. This is often a temporary solution.

Fig. 2.15. Adjusting a Key

The tone holes may not be even, or the pad cups may not be truly level. Leveling tone holes and pad cups requires additional steps and tools—something the novice may not wish to pursue. The method described above will seat the pads even if the pad cups are not level.

Often, two pads must close together. Seat each one separately, and then adjust them to the correct leveling height by adding or subtracting cork, or, if available, turning an adjustment screw.

Replacing a large number of pads requires the same procedures listed above but demands great patience. When disassembling the saxophone, identify and label all rods, pivot screws, and keys on a screw board (figure 2.16).

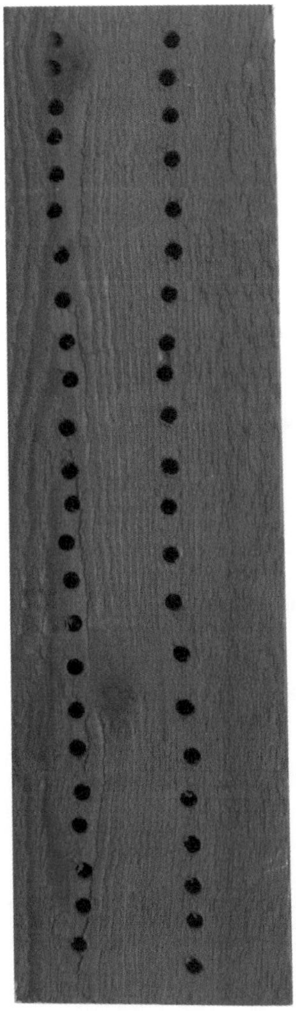

Fig. 2.16. Screw Board

Taking keys off a saxophone for a minor overhaul is the easy part. However, if pivot screws and rods get mixed together, the assembly after the overhaul suddenly becomes very difficult. A *screw board* (figure 2.16) is strongly recommended. These are available commercially or can be homemade. Obtain a small board, at least 4" x 6" or bigger, and drill numerous holes deep enough to hold pivot screws and rods. Divide the board into sections: left hand stack, right hand stack, bell keys, palm keys, C/E♭ combination, side lever keys, and octave key. As each screw or rod is removed, place it in the appropriate hole and specifically label it with a pencil (for example, RH, E key, etc.). Once all screws and rods are removed and placed in the board, tape them down so that they don't fall out. Assembling the keys back onto the saxophone will be far less intimidating and confusing as a result. The pencil markings can be erased when the project is completed.

Always set the work table over a bare floor, never over carpeting. Should one of those tiny pivot screws roll off the table, it can be located on a bare floor. It is no fun spending an hour on the floor examining carpet with a flashlight!

KEY ASSEMBLY ORDER

The following key assembly order applies to most saxophones. Slight deviations are found, depending on the manufacturer of the saxophone. The order listed below is suggested:

- G♯, C♯, B, B♭ spatula keys, then C♯ pad
- C/E♭ combination
- high F♯ key lever
- G♯ pad
- side B♭, C levers
- side B♭, C pads
- left-hand stack, including auxillary F♯ key
- high E key lever
- rest of high F3 key, including pad
- chromatic F♯ key
- G key
- octave key assembly
- auxillary F key attachment
- high D palm key
- high E♭, F palm keys together

KEY HEIGHTS

Often overlooked, key heights play a major role in tone production and intonation. If the key height is too low, the tone will be "stuffy," and pitches will be flat. If the key heights are too high, the opposite occurs. Commercial gauges that measure key height are available through repair tool suppliers (such as Ferree's in Michigan). Emilio Lyons, "The Sax Doctor," of Rayburn Music in Boston, has a simple but effective measuring device: a brand new, sharpened pencil. Emilio's pencil method was published in *The Saxophone Journal*, Vol. 17, No. 3. Use the pencil for alto saxophone keys in the following manner:

- Palm keys: sharpened end fits halfway between the point and paint
- B key: eraser barely fits between the key and tone hole
- Bis key: same
- A key: same
- G key: eraser is a tight fit but not as tight as above
- G♯ key: eraser fits easily
- Right-hand keys: eraser is a loose fit

For soprano, tenor, and baritone saxophones, add/subtract measurements approximating the list above. Keys can be lowered or raised by adding cork to the small "feet" underneath each key. Cork is preferable to felt because it takes longer to compress. There are some new synthetic materials, such as "tech cork" or "sheet Teflon," that are possibly even better than natural cork. It is best to remove the old cork or felt and replace it with the new material. It can then be sanded or filed to the proper thickness. A novice can successfully complete this procedure.

CHAPTER 3

Tone

*"To my ears, the saxophone is the most expressive of all wind instruments—
the one closest to the human voice."*
—Percy Grainger, Composer

Once suitable equipment is obtained, the focus should shift to tone production—
producing "your sound." Fundamentals are essential.

BREATHING

If you lie on your back, you can observe the natural rise and fall breathing
pattern of your lower abdomen. The involuntary muscles of the abdomen
are doing their job. This is the normal breathing process. Hand a saxophone
to a beginning saxophonist, though, and invariably, the natural breathing
process becomes unnatural: upper-chest breathing. Taking the breath in the
upper-chest area is harmful to good tone production and control. Upper-chest
breathing results in an insufficient air supply and a lack of tonal projection.
While inhaling, the shoulders often rise, with chest breathing, so identifying
this problem is easy.

The process of breathing for saxophone performance is the natural action of
normal, everyday breathing, with subtle differences. Air is taken in through the
mouth, rather than the nose, and exhalation is much longer than inhalation.
In addition, there is some flexing of the lower abdominal muscles to propel
the air at a controlled speed (support). During inhalation, the abdominal wall
expands forward, sideways, and backward, as the cavity fills from the bottom
up. The action of the diaphragm provides the lungs with enough room to also
expand.

Inhale:

- With the mouth slightly open, extend the stomach forward. Notice the feeling of the abdomen filling with air.
- Continue by expanding the rib cage. The lungs fill with air.
- Firm (flex) the abdominal muscles.

Exhale:

- Blow air through the mouth.
- Allow the stomach and rib cage to draw inward while still flexing the abdominal muscles.

Good breathing is enhanced by good posture and relaxation of the throat area. To introduce an understanding of the breathing process, start breathing through just the saxophone's neck and mouthpiece. Form the embouchure, take the breath through the sides of the mouth, expand, flex, and blow. Devise timing exercises to practice the sequence fully. For example, inhale two counts, set the embouchure, exhale and blow for four counts, then two and six, then two and eight, etc. Shorten the inhale count to one, and exhale and blow for four to twelve counts. When you are completely comfortable with this routine, add the rest of the saxophone, and practice long tones the same way. The "breathe and blow" process is:

Fig. 3.1. Breathe and Blow Process

Exercise 3.1. Breathing Practice

Here is a well-known exercise that demonstrates the breathing/support concept very well. Perform it until the breathing/support technique is automatic.

1. Lie flat on the ground, knees bent, feet on the floor.
2. Place a 10 pound weight (no more than that!) just below the ribs.
3. Extend the arms outward.
4. Push the weight up quickly while inhaling through the mouth.
5. Exhale slowly as the weight descends.
6. Maintain firm abdominal muscles.
7. Maintain an even, consistent air flow.
8. Start by inhaling for two counts, exhaling for four counts.
9. Gradually shorten inhaling and lengthening exhaling as described above.

An excellent way to transfer the breathing technique while practicing music can be achieved using the following sequence:

1. Place breath marks in the music.
2. Leisurely inhale/expand/flex/exhale, and play to the next breath mark. Then stop.
3. Repeat the breathing process again to the next breath mark, and continue on to all breath marks.
4. Repeat the sequence for several days, shortening the gap between breath marks, until breathing in tempo.

A common complaint from saxophonists is, "I feel like I'm full of air, but I'm gasping for air at the same time." As more and more air is inhaled in small amounts, the air is not expelled completely, creating an uncomfortable feeling. It becomes necessary to stop playing and exhale completely. To avoid this unpleasant sensation, exhale all residual air completely when there is an opportunity—for example, during a quarter rest or at the end of a phrase.

EMBOUCHURE

The embouchure is the connection to the saxophone. Producing a good tone requires the saxophonist and instrument to unite, allowing the reed to vibrate in a controlled yet free-blowing manner. There are countless descriptions published in numerous textbooks and journal articles regarding the saxophone embouchure. The simplified description, described below, should assist the beginner and the accomplished saxophonist equally well.

A teacher explains various techniques in different ways for different students. What works with one may not work with another. Remembering the roles of the upper lip, lower lip, upper teeth, lower teeth, corners, etc., may be too much to think about. Most people conceptualize "shape" rather easily, so a description of the shape of the embouchure may be more helpful.

A faulty embouchure can be characterized in many ways. Some of the frequent problems are:

- taking too little mouthpiece in the mouth
- using too much or too little red of the bottom lip on the reed
- escaping air from the corners
- a moving jaw, sideways or up and down
- corners pulled too far back into a "smile" shape
- jaw alignment—bottom jaw too far forward (underbite) or too far back (overbite)
- excessive bottom lip pressure on the reed (biting)

Just like a faulty embouchure can be characterized in many ways, so can a correct embouchure. Two well-documented descriptions of the embouchure have been articulated by Larry Teal and Joe Allard, two master teachers of the saxophone:

According to Larry Teal [3]:

- The bottom lip is rolled slightly over the bottom teeth.
- Half to two thirds of the red portion of the bottom lip covers the teeth.
- The upper teeth merely rest on top of the mouthpiece.
- The upper lip seals off the air.
- A well-functioning embouchure maintains equalized pressure in a circular fashion.
- The embouchure is like a rubber band around the mouthpiece.
- The embouchure is like a bag with drawstrings pulling it closed.
- The embouchure is like the letter O.

According to Joe Allard [4]:

- The bottom lip is flat, not curved.
- The head is level.
- The upper teeth exert a natural downward pressure on the mouthpiece.
- The upper lip exerts no pressure downward.
- The bottom lip is in the V position, placed directly behind the front teeth.
- The bottom lip rolls in and out, covering more or less of the reed depending on the register.

For some saxophonists, a combination of the Teal and Allard methods is preferred. Experiment with both methods to find the one that produces the best results.

Additional Thoughts Regarding Embouchure

The foundation of the embouchure is the chin. Stretch the skin by pulling the chin in a downward direction. Some refer to it as "pointing the chin" or "flattening the chin." Simultaneously pull your lower lip upward. A slight indentation will be noticeable just below the bottom lip. Many beginning and intermediate saxophonists place their top teeth and bottom lip incorrectly on the mouthpiece. Too little mouthpiece produces a small, pinched tone with a thin, sharp high register. Conversely, too much mouthpiece produces a harsh tone that is difficult to control. Insert a thin piece of paper between the mouthpiece and reed at the tip. Slide it further down the mouthpiece facing until it stops. This is the "breakpoint" where the reed separates from

[3] Teal, Larry. *The Art of Saxophone Playing*. Evanston: Summy-Birchard Inc., 1963.
[4] Liebman, David. *Developing a Personal Saxophone Sound*. Medfield: Dorn Publications Inc., 1989.

the mouthpiece facing/curve. The top teeth and bottom lip should be aligned at this breakpoint for maximum flexibility and sound quality. This placement will suit the great majority of saxophonists.

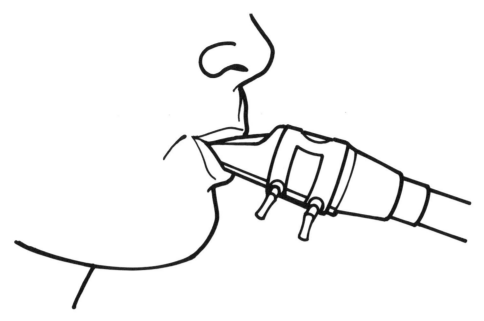

Fig. 3.2. Embouchure

To produce the many nuances needed for playing jazz, such as sub-toning, ghosting, etc., saxophonists are required to move the jaw into unorthodox positions. Other nuances require more flexibility and changes in the normal embouchure to produce these specialized effects.

It is advisable to practice embouchure formation and control in the early stages by playing on the mouthpiece and neck alone and using a mirror. Be sure that the mouthpiece is in the correct tuning position on the neck cork, and then play a series of long tones. Make sure the chin is parallel to the floor. The pitch produced should be an A-flat concert pitch, a minor sixth above middle C on the piano (written as F on the fifth ledger line for an E-flat saxophone).

"Biting" is the number one embouchure problem and is often a result of taking too little mouthpiece in the mouth. Temporary remedial work may be necessary using a "double lip" embouchure, similar to that of an oboist. Play in the middle and upper octaves with *both* lips covering the teeth. This technique softens the bottom lip, eliminates biting, and requires the corners of the mouth to exert more control. The tone will likely noticeably improve in quality using this technique, although it may be decidedly uncomfortable at first. Play a one octave scale in the middle register, ascending and descending, with the double lip version. Form the embouchure again, single lip, simulating the "feel" of the double-lip embouchure, and play the scale again. Repeat this short exercise for a week, and the biting problem can be eliminated permanently.

Another approach useful for determining the correct amount of lower-lip pressure on the reed is shown in figure 3.3. The diagram indicates five different levels of lip pressure, with 5 representing maximum pressure on the reed and 1 representing the least. Play a series of pitches at each level of pressure, and note the differences in tone quality at each number. Begin with 5 and proceed to 1, gradually reducing the lip pressure on the reed.

Note that a level of 2 to 3 allows the reed to vibrate freely and produces a full but controlled tone. A 5 produces a squeezed, pinched quality, and 1 is flat in pitch with a lack of center and control.

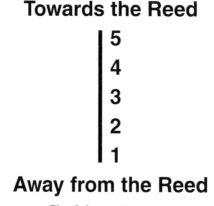

Towards the Reed

5

4

3

2

1

Away from the Reed

Fig. 3.3. Lip Pressure

The primary purpose of the embouchure is to control the reed yet also allow it to vibrate. Too many students apply the "jaw-bite" method, where the top teeth serve as an anchor and the bottom lip presses upward too firmly into the reed. When the amount of pressure is correct, certain pitches can be produced using the mouthpiece and reed alone. Be sure to hold the mouthpiece parallel to the floor, and don't cover the end. The pitches should be:

- soprano: C two octaves above middle C on the piano
- alto: A one octave plus a major sixth above middle C
- tenor: G one octave plus a perfect fifth above middle C
- baritone: D one octave plus a major second above middle C

If the sustained pitch is higher, there is too much jaw-bite pressure and not enough control maintained by the corners of the lips. The remedial technique using the double-lip embouchure relaxes the pressure.

Perform this exercise the first thing in the practice session, for just a few minutes. It may take time, but eventually, the results become well worth the effort.

THROAT SHAPES

In speech, the tongue moves to different positions to articulate vowels and consonants, altering the shape of the oral cavity. Changing the shape of the oral cavity also alters a saxophone tone. Various pedagogical sources suggest the use of "oh," "aw," and other vowel shapes for playing the saxophone.

Consider using "ee," as in the word "even." Master teacher and saxophonist Joe Allard believed this throat shape to be superior to all others. There are many disciples of Allard who also believe in this principle. By employing the "ee" throat shape, the tongue is placed in the center of the oral cavity, maximizing the velocity and direction of the airstream in the cavity. An added advantage is that the "ee" shape facilitates the production of overtones and the extended range. However, compare it to other recommended throat shapes to determine which one produces the best results.

TAPERING

Sustained musical tones are shaped like a football. There is a symmetrical tapering at both the beginning and ending of a tone. Think of it as a gradual crescendo, however long or short, before maximum volume is reached. A decrescendo follows until the tone ends. The ability to release a tone with a controlled taper is fundamental to good tone production and phrasing.

To taper a pitch, simply change the throat shape from "ee" to "rr," as in saying the word "ear." The longer the "rr" shape is maintained and the air is in motion, the longer the taper.

At a saxophone conference, years ago, an American university saxophone professor taught a master class saxophone lesson with a European student before a large audience at a World Saxophone Congress convention. The student did not speak English. While performing his piece, the student consistently "chopped" the ends of his notes by abruptly closing his throat or touching the reed. The result was a very unmusical release. The American professor, unable to communicate with the student through language, strolled over to a closet door. He blasted a sudden and very loud note on his saxophone while violently yanking the door open with his hand and then abruptly stopped the tone while slamming it shut. The professor then played the same note with a beautifully tapered crescendo and decrescendo by opening and closing the door very slowly. The simple but effective demonstration was all that was needed to instruct the student on the fine art of tapering. The master class resumed, and the student successfully tapered his pitches from that point on.

Any pitch before a rest, a breath, or at the end of a phrase should be tapered. To practice tapering, set a metronome at a slow tempo, and play scales or intervals, tapering each pitch within six beats, then four, then two, then one. The "ee" should gradually change to "rr" as the airspeed slows.

CREATING DARK AND BRIGHT TIMBRES

Through manipulation of tone color (timbre), tone quality can be modified to express the musical intent of a musical passage. The performer can alter the timbre slightly to reflect the level of intensity of the music. In some contemporary compositions, the composer clearly labels the music with symbols representing bright versus dark timbres. For example, a plus sign (+) would indicate bright while a minus sign (–) would indicate dark. An accelerando combined with a rapid succession of notes might dictate a brighter tone while a serene, lyrical, soft passage might suggest a darker tone.

Two techniques will create dark and bright timbres:
1. For a brighter tone, adjust the corners of the lips from the basic embouchure by pulling them back slightly into more of a "smile." The bottom lip stretches and adds an edge to the tone. Conversely, moving the corners forward focuses the tone, producing a darker quality.
2. Add and subtract keys. Closing additional keys will "cover" the sound while opening keys produces slightly more brilliance. Play a high C-sharp, and add the right-hand keys one at a time. As each key is added, the timbre becomes increasingly darker sounding, as well as flatter in pitch.

Many notes on the saxophone can be altered this way. There are just a few possibilities to brighten a tone by opening keys, however. Play high A, open the G-sharp key, and the tone becomes somewhat brighter and sharper. Since closing/opening keys also affects intonation, an adjustment with lip pressure may be necessary to compensate.

Experiment with the use of dark and bright timbres to enhance the expressiveness of a musical phrase.

NECK AND MOUTHPIECE PRACTICE

Beginners or those undergoing an embouchure change should spend a few minutes practicing each day with just the neck and mouthpiece. By removing the weight of the saxophone and any finger movement, it is easier to focus on breathing, air support, embouchure formation, articulation, and vocalization. This is particularly true regarding embouchure and top-teeth placement. Typically, most beginning or intermediate saxophonists place their top teeth on the mouthpiece too close to the tip rail. As a result, the tone is pinched and sharp in the upper register. Learning to move the front teeth further away from the tip rail and to the "breakpoint" is more easily achieved using just the neck and mouthpiece, in the beginning.

VIBRATO

Composer Percy Grainger referred to the saxophone as the instrument most similar to the human voice, possessing a singing quality. Like the human voice, the saxophone tone usually includes a tone-enhancing vibrato. Integrated with the use of dynamics, vibrato becomes a powerful emotional tool for expressive performance and individual styles.

The physical approach to producing a saxophone vibrato is a jaw/lip movement that permits the straight tone to dip slightly flat and return to the straight tone but not above it. It is a pitch variation vibrato. This method of production is different from any of the other woodwind instruments. When performed correctly, the movement of the lip/jaw is so slight that an observer may not be able to detect it, visually.

The darker lines in figure 3.4 represent straight tones without vibrato. Note that the straight tones are in the "middle" of the pitch (see figure 3.3., level 2 to 3 lip pressure). The " ⑆⑆ " shapes shown represent the lip/jaw action. Relaxing the lip and jaw produces a pitch that dips flat and returns to the lip pressure normally used to produce a straight tone. Incorrect vibrato is produced by pinching the reed above the straight tone (figure 3.3, level 5 lip pressure). The center of the pitch should be maintained at all times.

(a) Correct Vibrato   (b) Incorrect Vibrato

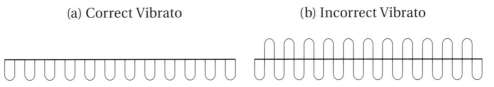

Fig. 3.4. Vibrato

Once you have enough control to play the entire range (excluding altissimo) with a well-centered tone, it is time to begin the process of learning vibrato. The concept of tone plays a major role in developing a musical vibrato. All saxophonists should listen to great performers, both classical and jazz, and not necessarily just saxophonists. Much can be learned from violinists and vocalists. Vibrato is very stylistic and differs from one artist to the next, but there are enough similarities to contribute to the learning process. Imitation is a terrific way to develop vibrato.

JAZZ VS. CLASSICAL VIBRATO

The differences between a classical vibrato and jazz vibrato are best learned through listening and copying styles. Essentially, a classical vibrato is part of the tone and is continuous from the start of the pitch, whereas a contemporary jazz vibrato begins with a straight tone and gradually changes into wide and slow pulses, more of an ornament to the tone. There are as many styles of vibrato as there are genres. Rock, soul, pop, dixieland, swing, bebop, etc., are characteristically different.

VIBRATO DEVELOPMENT EXERCISES

Initially, control of vibrato is achieved by practicing "measured" vibrato. This mechanical approach develops precise depth and speed. The following exercises should be practiced until complete command is achieved, and it should remain as part of a daily warm-up routine.

The approximate speed of a measured vibrato in performance for alto saxophone is:

- 3 pulses per beat at 108 bpm or
- 4 pulses per beat at 80 bpm or
- 5 pulses per beat at 63 bpm or
- 6 pulses per beat at 54 bpm

For soprano, the speed is slightly faster, about 4 pulses per beat at 84 bpm. For tenor, about 4 pulses per beat at 72 bpm, and for baritone about 4 pulses per beat at 66 bpm. These numbers are subject to individual saxophonist's style. For tenor and baritone, the depth is correspondingly wider. Practice the following developmental exercises. Major scales that extend for two octaves are used for the examples. For variety, also play them descending.

To maintain control of vibrato and generate the proper sound, the width should decrease gradually when ascending to the higher notes, similar to a violin vibrato:

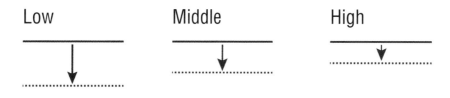

Fig. 3.5. Vibrato Width

In the following exercises, give each note one vibrato pulse.

Exercise 3.2. Vibrato Exercise 1: Quarter Notes

Begin by practicing these vibrato exercises as written. Then, transpose them to all other major keys, moving through the circle of fifths. Gradually increase the speed, up to at least 160 bpm.

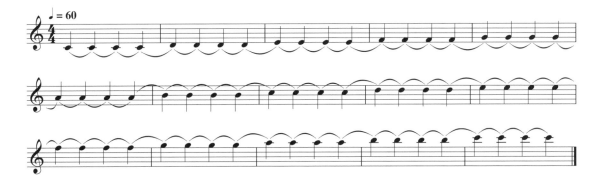

Fig. 3.6. Vibrato Exercise

Exercise 3.3. Vibrato Exercise 2: Eighth Notes

Begin by practicing these vibrato exercises as written. Then, transpose them to all other major keys, moving through the circle of fifths. Gradually increase the speed up to at least 160 bpm.

Fig. 3.7. Vibrato Exercise 2: Eighth Notes

Exercise 3.4. Vibrato Exercise 3: Sixteenth Notes

Begin by practicing these vibrato exercises as written. Then, transpose them to all other major keys, moving through the circle of fifths. For alto saxophone, 80 bpm is the goal.

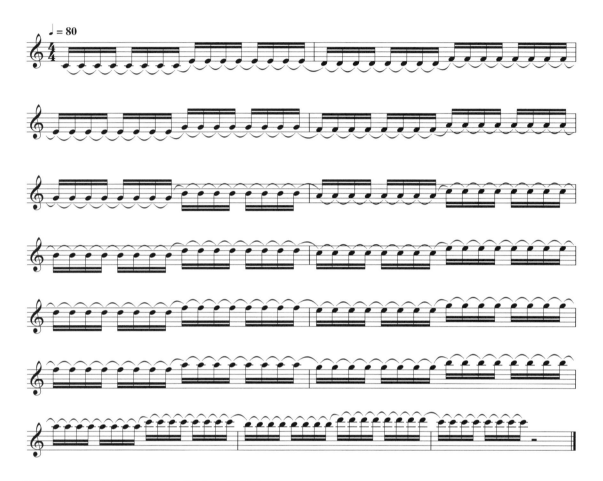

Fig. 3.8. Vibrato Exercise 3: Sixteenth Notes

Exercise Variations: Also play these exercises descending. Gradually widen the intervals to fourths, fifths, etc.

VIBRATO AND PITCH

It is possible that vibrato may affect the center of a pitch too much, causing intonation problems and contributing to an overall lack of control of vibrato speed and width. The center of the pitch must be secure at all times. A way to remedy uncontrolled pitch center is to set the metronome at the current tempo, play 2 counts straight tone, 4 counts with vibrato, 2 counts straight tone as shown below, using any scale or arpeggio. Hearing the centered pitch of the straight tone before beginning the vibrato often solves the problem.

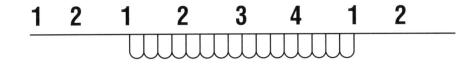

Fig. 3.9. Vibrato

Once measured vibrato is fully controlled, then the process of playing "unmeasured" vibrato begins. This is a shift from the mechanical version to a more lyrical, musical one. Using any etude or solo, set a metronome tempo at 80 bpm. Arbitrarily, place a fermata over several notes, spaced apart. Change the rhythm by playing all eighth notes until reaching the fermata notes. All the eighth notes are straight tones, and the fermata notes are played with a sustained vibrato. Continue the same pattern to the next fermata, and so on. Begin the vibrato immediately on the fermata notes rather than adding it gradually. Then play the music as written, rhythmically, and again place vibrato on the fermata notes. Finally, erase the fermatas, and play the music again, as written, making an effort to use vibrato on any note of suitable duration. After a week or two of practice, it becomes quite comfortable using vibrato in a natural and musical way.

Vibrato use can be very expressive when applied to dynamics and tempo changes. For example, use a vibrato speed of about 66 bpm on a metronome for slow tempos at *p* or *mp* dynamic levels. As the tempo increases or the dynamic level is *mf* or stronger, increase the vibrato speed to 72 to 80 bpm. Generally, faster vibrato adds intensity while slower vibrato reduces intensity.

INTONATION

"My saxophone was tuned at the factory." This is an old joke and just that—a joke. The perfectly-in-tune saxophone has never been manufactured. However, some models are certainly better than others, regarding intonation. The burden of playing in tune still lies with the saxophonist. The effects of a beautiful tone, fabulous technique, and lyrical phrases are ruined by poor intonation.

Pay attention to proper key heights. Review the information on page 32.

There are three ways to improve intonation on a saxophone. One is by altering "voicing." Similar to a vocalist, by moving the larynx up or down, a saxophonist can modify pitch. It is remarkable how much a pitch can be altered using this method. Finger a high B, and voice the pitch downward by lowering the larynx, and then bring it back up. There is a great deal of variation where the pitch B can be voiced. Be aware that the lower pitches on a saxophone have much less voicing flexibility. As previously mentioned, with correct embouchure and voicing, the pitch produced on an alto mouthpiece should be an "A" concert, one ledger line above the treble staff.

On the mouthpiece, using a piano as a guide, "voice" downwards by half steps to A-flat, then G. Go up by half steps from A to B-flat, then to B. At first, the workable range may be two pitches or possibly none at all. Someone who has practiced this routine daily for a long time might be able to produce a full octave.

Another method is closing and opening keys. Generally, closing keys will lower a pitch, and opening keys will raise a pitch. For example, second-space A is raised by opening the G-sharp key. Middle F or F-sharp is raised by opening the D-sharp key. Lowering the high C-sharp is accomplished by adding one or more keys in the right-hand stack. Fourth line D is lowered by adding the low B key. It cannot be done on all saxophone pitches, however. Experiment with individual pitches, fingerings, and an electronic tuner.

Saxophonists who play in tune employ both methods. The results are predictable and stable intonation.

The third method is monitoring temperature. Cold temperatures lower pitch, while hot temperatures raise pitch. Even if the air temperature is moderate—72 degrees Fahrenheit for example—the saxophonist's airstream will warm the air within the bore, and the pitch will go sharp. During a sixteen-measure rest, the air inside the bore cools and the pitch drops. Therefore, during a performance, the saxophonist is compelled to push and pull the mouthpiece on the neck as needed to play in tune. During long rests, it is advisable to periodically blow warm air through the saxophone.

Tracking Intonation

In order to acquire solid intonation, you must know and track the intonation tendencies of each note on your saxophone: which pitches are sharp or flat and by how much. Figure 3.11 is an intonation chart, which you can use to track your instrument's intonation. Update this chart every few months to monitor progress. It is best to have someone assist you with this process, but you can also do it alone.

After a thorough warm-up, tune to an exact A440, indicated on the chart with an * on the pitch F♯. Mark a dot on the center line and then proceed downward by half steps. Play with a straight tone, about mezzo-forte, and continue marking each note on the chart as to how many cents it is sharp or flat. If performing the test alone, first play the pitch, *then* look at the tuner. After playing one octave, tune again to A440 to keep an accurate reference point, then resume downward towards low B-flat. After reaching low B-flat, tune one more time to A440, and then proceed upwards starting on F♯ again until all pitches are marked on the chart. Now connect the dots, and a blueprint of your personal pitch tendencies emerges. Like voiceprints and fingerprints, it is unique to the individual instrument.

Intonation Chart

Cents Flat	30	25	20	15	10	5		5	10	15	20	25	30	Cents Sharp
F♯														
F														
E														
D♯														
D														
C♯														
C														
B														
A♯														
A														
G♯														
G														
F♯*														
F														
E														
D♯														
D														
C♯														
C														
B														
A♯														
A														
G♯														
G														
F♯														
F														
E														
D♯														
D														
C♯														
C														
B														
B♭														

Fig. 3.10. Intonation Chart

After comparing numerous intonation charts, a typical profile emerged:

Cents Flat	30	25	20	15	10	5	5	10	15	20	25	30	Cents Sharp
F♯								*					
F									*				
E										*			
D♯									*				
D									*				
C♯											*		
C								*					
B									*				
A♯								*					
A									*				
G♯								*					
G								*					
F♯						tuning	note						
F								*					
E									*				
D♯									*				
D										*			
C♯			*										
C				*									
B					*								
A♯						*							
A						*							
G♯						*							
G						*							
F♯						tuning	note						
F						*							
E						*							
D♯						*							
D				*									
C♯						*							
C						*							
B								*					
B♭									*				

Fig. 3.11. Typical Intonation Chart Profile

With time, daily practice on the chromatic scale, and a tuner, a saxophonist can improve intonation problems. The intonation chart will eventually show more pitches near the center line. No one plays dead center all the time. A reasonable goal is to be within 5 to 10 cents on all pitches.

The knowledge then has to be applied in musical situations. If other members of an ensemble are unable to play in tune, the burden may fall upon the informed saxophonist to do the adjusting—in effect, play *out* of tune in order to play *in* tune.

The "Tuning in Fifths" exercise is another way you can improve intonation. It can be practiced with another saxophonist, alone with a sustained keyboard tone, or alone with a chromatic tuner. The perfect fifth interval works particularly well for adjusting intonation on specific pitches because it is so easy to hear. Try to adjust pitches by "voicing" rather than tightening and loosening lip pressure.

As mentioned, *voicing* is the ability to move the larynx up and down like a vocalist does to sing different pitches. This requires flexibility, and it takes practice to acquire it. Start by placing the tongue in an "ee" position, as in the word "even." The tongue is in the center of the oral cavity with the sides close to the top molars. This position facilitates tonguing, creates a centered tone, and is advantageous for extended register studies. There is more information on voicing in the section on "The Extended Range."

Begin by tuning to A440, if using a chromatic tuner or keyboard. If another saxophonist is participating, both should tune to a concert A and each other. Play at mezzo-forte with a straight tone. Stay in rhythm on the whole notes, and try to tune each note within four beats.

If both saxophonists are familiar with their intonation tendencies, the fifths exercise will be more successful. Both players must anticipate the next pitch and adjust before playing it. Obviously, when playing with a keyboard or tuner, the entire burden is on the person.

Exercise 3.5. Tuning in Fifths: Whole Notes

First, practice this exercise as written. When you are ready, double the tempo, as if you were playing half notes. Then double it again, as if they were quarter notes. As you speed it up, pitch adjustments will have to be made more quickly.

Fig. 3.12. Turning in Fifths: Whole Notes

THE EXTENDED RANGE

Sigurd Rascher, the classical saxophone pioneer, was performing in the altissimo register in the 1930s. Since then, saxophonists have become adept at performing in the extended range. Students in high school and college are playing the third register as though it is the normal range of the saxophone. The bottom line is that every saxophonist who intends to play the standard classical saxophone literature or who aspires to play jazz, rock, blues, etc., absolutely must be able to conquer the high notes. The exercises for mastery of the extended range are beneficial to tone development as well as technique, and therefore are included within this section.

The process of learning the extended range is methodical and requires patience and determination. In the appendix, there is a partial listing of published texts that have been widely adopted. All of these books are highly recommended.

INTRODUCTION TO THE OVERTONE SERIES

All pitches vibrate at a precise frequency of cycles per second that determines the highness or lowness of that pitch. For example, tuning note concert A vibrates at 440 cycles per second, also known as Hertz (Hz). One octave higher, A vibrates at 880 cycles per second. The saxophone produces a fundamental tone. Harmonics generated from the fundamental determines the timbre. Because of the varying strengths of these harmonics, different instruments produce characteristically different tones.

It is easiest to describe the overtone series in terms of a string. If a vibrating string (the fundamental) is divided into two equal parts by touching the exact center, a harmonic—also termed an *overtone*—is created. Each of the two halves of the string vibrates twice as fast, producing an octave. If the string is then divided into thirds, each portion or partial of the string produces a perfect fifth interval. Four divisions is a perfect fourth, five divisions is major third, etc.

The fundamental is also called the first harmonic. The octave above is the second harmonic, also the first overtone. The perfect fifth above that is the third harmonic and second overtone, etc.

The following identifies the interval structure of the pitch A (fundamental) and the harmonic or overtone series through eight partials:

- fundamental on A @ 220 Hz
- first overtone on A @ 440 Hz, octave
- second overtone on E @ 660 Hz, perfect fifth
- third overtone on A @ 880 Hz, perfect fourth
- fourth overtone on C-sharp @ 1100 Hz, major third
- fifth overtone on E @ 1320 Hz, minor third
- sixth overtone on G @ 1540 Hz, minor third
- seventh overtone on A @ 1760 Hz, major second

The harmonic (or overtone) series continues beyond the example above, but for practical application to saxophone practice, the fundamental plus seven overtones is sufficient.

THE OVERTONE SERIES

Practicing the overtone series on the saxophone provides the groundwork for controlling voicing by building larynx flexibility. It also improves embouchure control and air support and is the "gateway" to the extended range. Shown below are overtones built on fundamentals B-flat, B, C, and C-sharp:

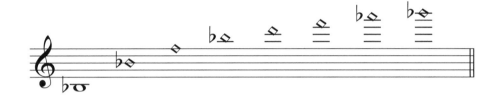

Fig. 3.13. Overtones of B-Flat

Fig. 3.14. Overtones of B, C, C-Sharp

BUILDING FLEXIBILITY

In the earlier references to voicing, it was emphasized that the ability to move the larynx, similar to a vocalist, is paramount to good intonation. Voicing also pertains to developing the extended range. A few preliminary exercises in voicing flexibility are presented here. Key points to remember are:

- Use the "ee" throat cavity syllable, as advocated by master teacher Joe Allard.
- Use a secure, controlled embouchure. No biting allowed.
- Use a straight tone, no vibrato.

Exercise 3.6. Overtone Exercises

Without Octave Key

Play overtone intervals (diamond-head notes) *without the octave key* by voicing higher. It may help to start them with the air, rather than the tongue. Try using space between pitches rather than connecting them. As previously mentioned, the possible range extends higher than the example shown below. Play about an *mf* volume, and don't force it.

Fig. 3.15. Overtones with Voicings Exercise

With Octave Key

Again using figure 3.15, play the lower notes with normal fingerings, but this time, play the diamond-head notes by *adding the octave key*. While pressing the octave key, voice downward to the lower notes.

Exercise 3.7. Overtone Exercise to Octave and Fifth

Using fundamentals C, B, B♭, B, C, C♯, voice to the octave and perfect fifth above. C is chosen as the starting point because, for most people, it is the easiest to produce. Do not use the octave key.

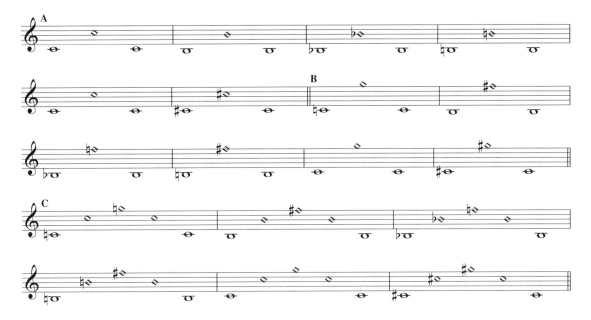

Fig. 3.16. Overtone Exercise to Octave and Fifth

Exercise 3.8. Normal/Voiced Overtone Practice

Use the normal fingering on the first and second notes, and voice the overtone (diamond-shaped notes).

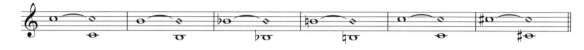

Fig. 3.17. Normal/Voiced Overtone Practice

Exercise 3.9. Voiced Overtone/Normal Practice

This is the reverse of exercise 3.8.

Fig. 3.18. Voiced Overtone/Normal Practice

Exercise 3.10. Matching Practice 1

Match the normal fingering to the overtone with no space between them.

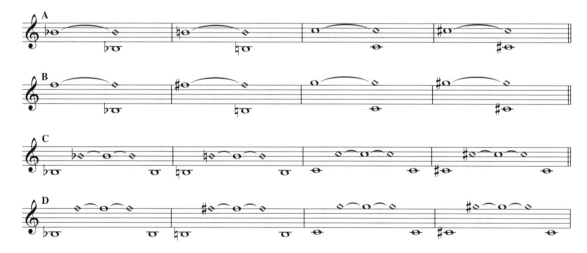

Fig. 3.19. Matching Practice 1

Exercise 3.11. Matching Practice 2

Continue matching the normal fingering with the overtone.

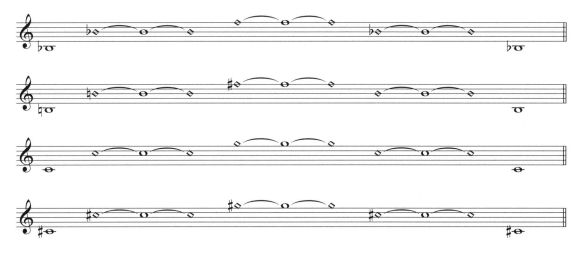

Fig. 3.20. Matching Practice 2

Exercise 3.12. Matching Practice 3

Reverse the pattern.

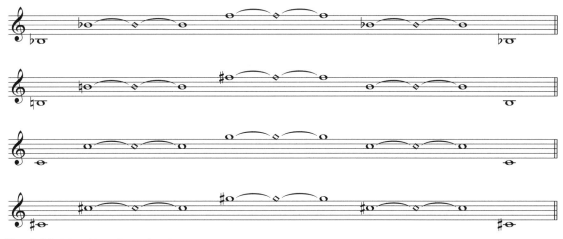

Fig. 3.21. Matching Practice 3

Exercise 3.13. Overtone Exercise with Perfect Fourth

Add the perfect fourth to the overtone pattern.

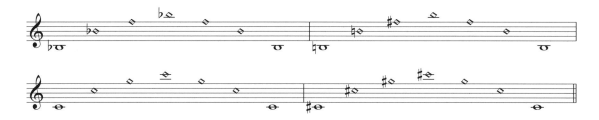

Fig. 3.22. Overtone Exercise with Perfect Fourth

Exercise 3.14. Random Overtone Sequence

Practice this random overtone pattern as written, and then alter the sequence. For example: 2-5-3-1-6-4, etc.

Fig. 3.23. Random Overtone Sequence

Exercise 3.15. Voicing Down Half Steps

Finger the first note. Without changing the fingering, voice downward a half step (X-shaped note).

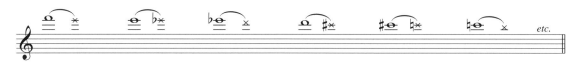

Fig. 3.24. Voicing Down Half Steps

After devoting considerable time to practicing the overtone exercises, begin putting together your personal collection of altissimo fingerings. It is advisable to have more than one fingering for each note, since it provides options for smoother technique or matching of timbre. Intonation is also a factor because there is a great degree of variance among fingerings.

Begin with simple arpeggios and scales in all keys, played very slowly at first to gain a sense of how to voice these notes and to improve the quality of sound and intonation. There are many scale and arpeggio books that are useful. Just transpose the notes an octave higher. Also, playing simple children's songs is an excellent way to judge your command of the higher notes. Some key points to remember are:

- Don't overblow or force the tone.
- Work for the best possible tone.
- Repeat the pattern several times.
- Devote just a few minutes of each practice session to the altissimo register.
- Be patient and persistent.

The extended range fingering chart is for the alto saxophone only. The indicated fingerings represent only a few of the numerous possibilities. Note that soprano, tenor, and baritone fingerings are different. Consult any of the recommended extended range texts in the appendix for those fingerings.

EXTENDED RANGE FINGERING CHART

Alto Saxophone: octave key on all fingerings; p = palm key

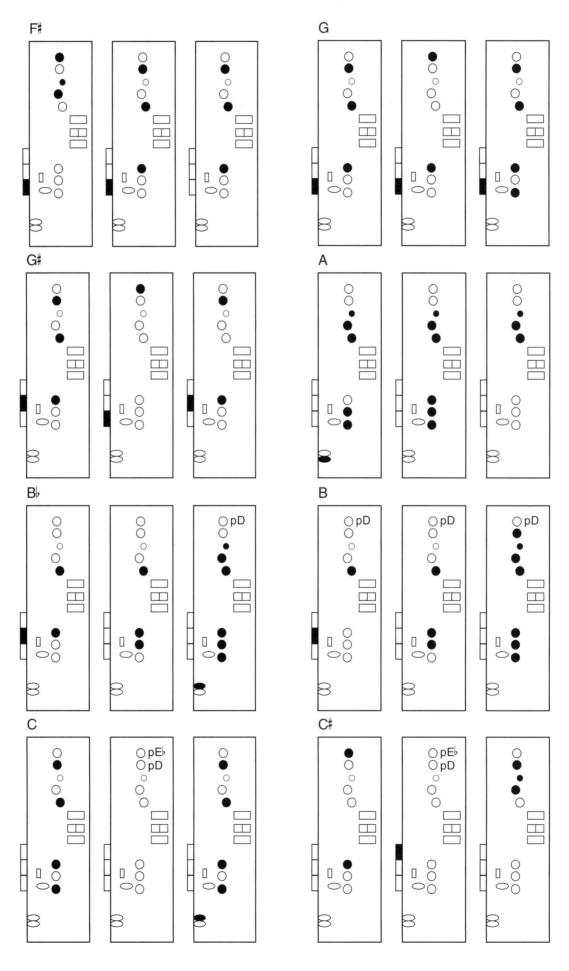

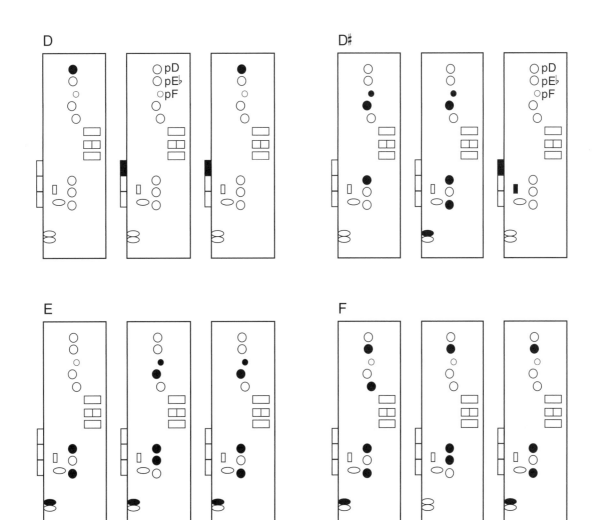

Fig. 3.25. Extended Range

Add your own:

Additional Fingerings

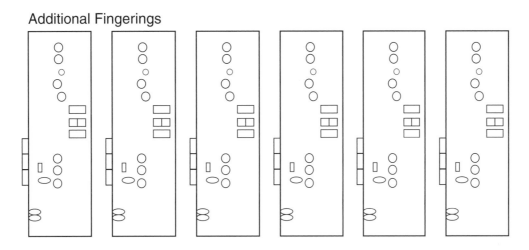

Fig. 3.26. Extended Range Additional

CHAPTER 4

Technique

"Patience is the greatest of all virtues."
—Cato the Elder, Roman Orator

Building a solid, reliable technique is a long process achieved only through dedication, effort, and patience. Without correct fundamentals, the process becomes much longer with no guarantee of success.

POSTURE

The saxophone is played both standing and sitting, so you should practice both ways. Fundamentally sound posture with a saxophone is identical to good posture without one. If standing, your weight is evenly distributed on both feet, knees slightly bent, an erect but not stiff upper body, and shoulders down and relaxed. Be sure that the neck strap is cinched enough that your chin is parallel to the floor and the mouthpiece is at an even level with the embouchure. Imagine a saxophone hanging from a string, and you simply walk up to it and begin to play it. There is no need to add tension in the body by contorting your posture in any way. There is a natural bending of the torso to read the music stand, of course.

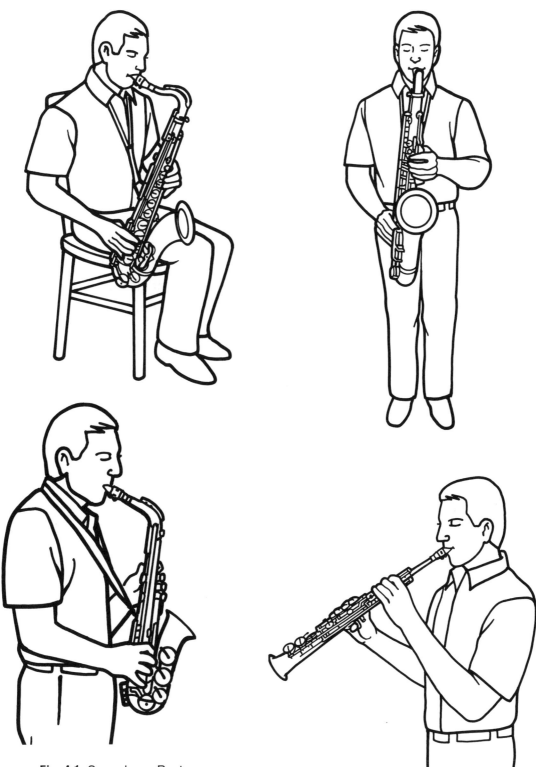

Fig. 4.1. Saxophone Posture

When sitting, the options are to hold your saxophone to the side or in front of your body, for alto saxophone. Tenor and baritone are always played to the side. If the alto is in front, the neck strap should bring the mouthpiece to the embouchure with no bending of the neck downward or upward. The chin is parallel to the floor. The back is relaxed but straight and away from the back of the chair. In the side position, the chin is also parallel to the floor, but it is usually necessary to turn the mouthpiece on the neck cork slightly to keep your head centered.

HAND POSITION

There are four "control points" that allow your fingers to move quickly and efficiently on the keys:

1. right thumb in the thumb hook
2. left thumb at a 45 degree angle to the body of the saxophone (imagine the thumb rest as a clock; the thumb is pointed at 2:00)
3. the neck strap
4. embouchure/mouthpiece connection

The 2:00 left thumb position is critical and cannot be emphasized enough. Many saxophonists point at 3:00, which pulls the left hand away from the palm keys. The left wrist will bend, and it is impossible to push the palm keys. At 2:00, the left wrist is straight, and you can actually feel the palm keys in the fingers. There is minimal movement, which means improved technique. On some vintage saxophones, the octave key may be placed at 12:00 or 1:00. In order to keep the left wrist straight, press the octave key with the side of the thumb.

Keeping the 2:00 position is difficult for those who have done differently for a long time. Old habits can be hard to correct. Try attaching a 6 inch ruler to the inside of your left arm, from the middle of the palm, past the wrist and up the forearm. A couple of thick rubber bands will hold it in place. The ruler prevents the bending of the wrist and helps maintain optimum left arm/hand position. It is also impossible to ignore!

The fingers are relaxed, with both knuckles slightly bent, similar to how you would type on a computer keyboard. Place your hand on a softball, gripping it with all fingers and thumb. You now have perfect hand/finger position to play the saxophone.

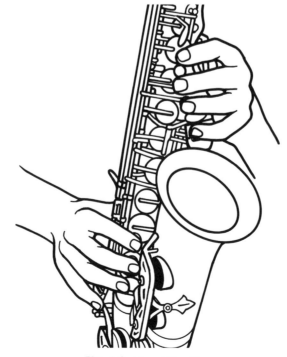

Fig. 4.2. Hand Position

The fingering chart below includes the standard fingerings for the chromatic scale, spelled enharmonically from low B-flat to high F-sharp. Included in the chart are some alternate fingerings. In some French publications, alternate fingerings are notated as C1 (palm D key), C2 (palm E-flat key), C3 (right side high E key), C4 (palm key F), and C5 (high F-sharp key).

Some pitches have multiple fingerings. There are variances in timbre, intonation, and ease of use among these fingerings. Based on these considerations, choose the one most appropriate for the particular musical passage.

FINGERING CHART

ok = octave key

p = palm key

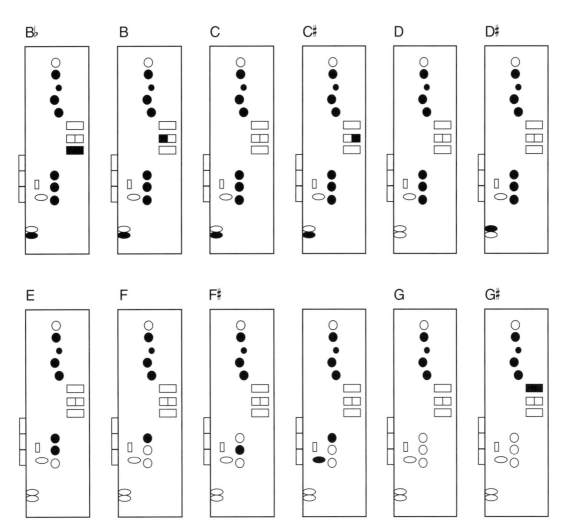

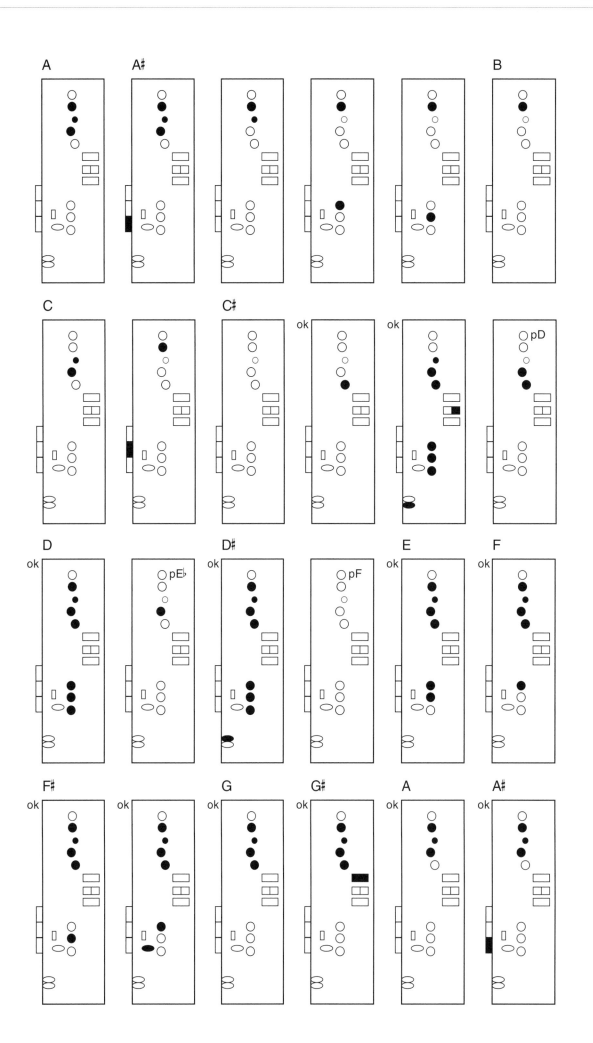

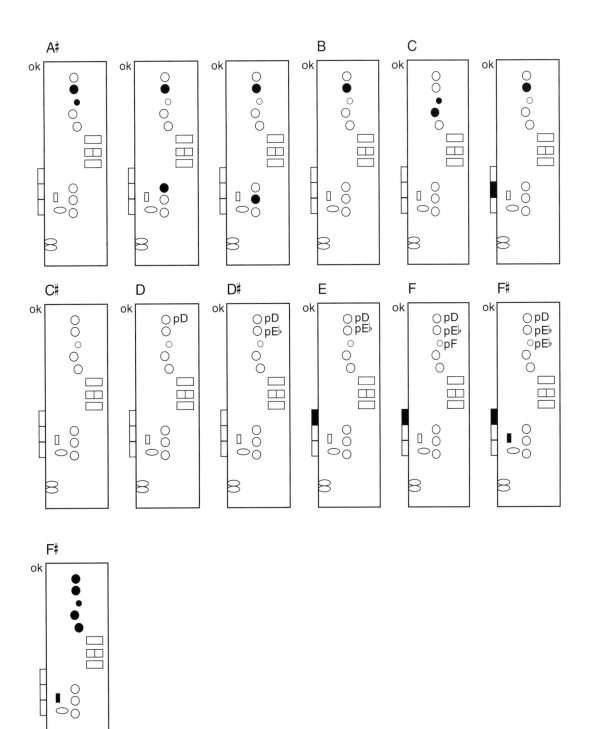

Fig. 4.3. Fingering Chart

TRILLS

The musical rule for trills is to trill to the note above, based on the key signature, unless notated otherwise. For example, if the key signature has two sharps and the note B is marked with a trill, trill to C-sharp. If the composer intends a trill from B to C-natural, a natural sign is placed above the trill sign as shown in figure 4.4.

Accidentals for trills placed above the trill sign supersede the key signature rule.

Fig. 4.4. Trills

Trills are considered musical ornaments. When executing any trill, consider its musical importance to the phrase, tempo, and dynamic level.

The volume and speed of the trill should reflect the mood of the music at that point:

intense = a faster, louder trill

calm = a slower, softer trill.

HALF-STEP TRILL CHART

In the following half-step fingering chart, the trill key is indicated by the straight line.

ok = octave key

p = palm key

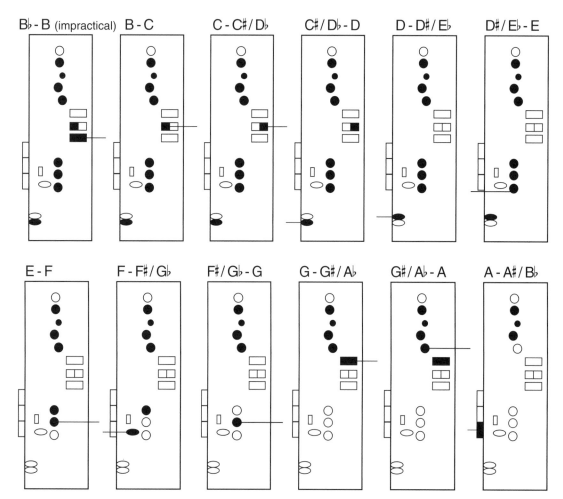

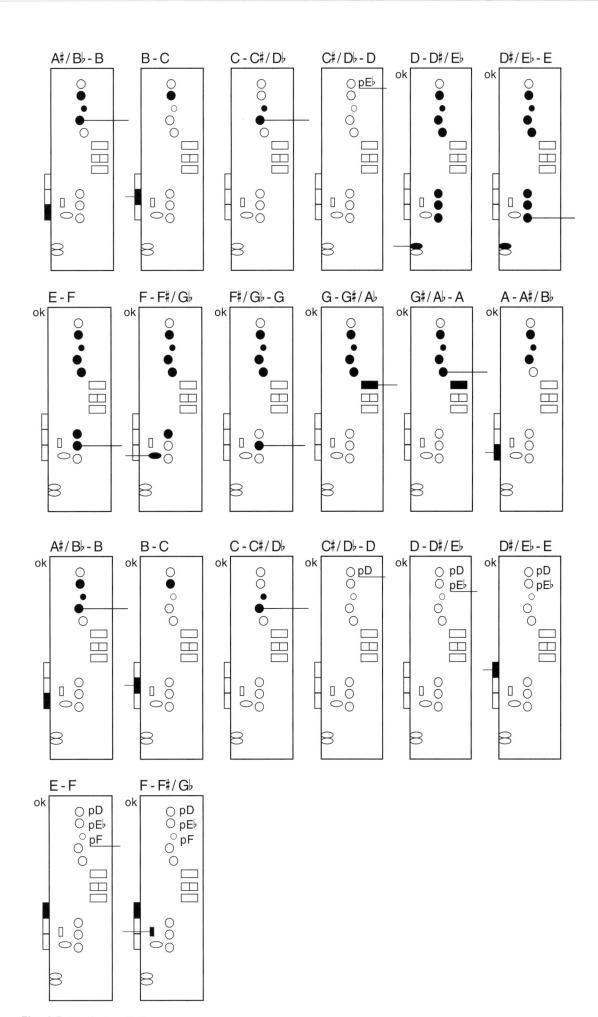

Fig. 4.5. Half-step Trills

WHOLE-STEP TRILL CHART

In the following whole-step fingering chart, the trill key is indicated by the straight line.

ok = octave key

p = palm key

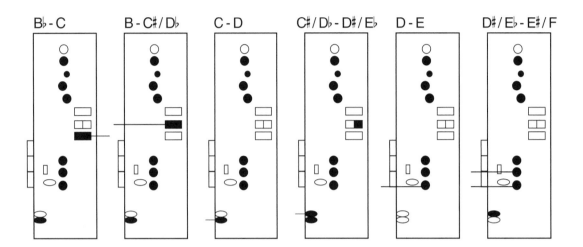

B♭ - C   B - C♯/D♭   C - D   C♯/D♭ - D♯/E♭   D - E   D♯/E♭ - E♯/F

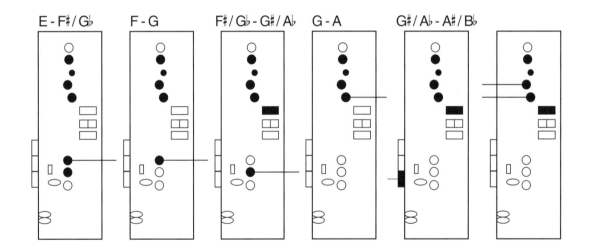

E - F♯/G♭   F - G   F♯/G♭ - G♯/A♭   G - A   G♯/A♭ - A♯/B♭

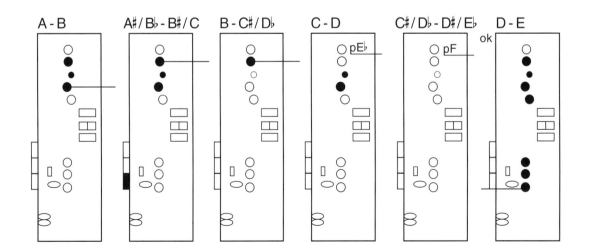

A - B   A♯/B♭ - B♯/C   B - C♯/D♭   C - D   C♯/D♭ - D♯/E♭   D - E

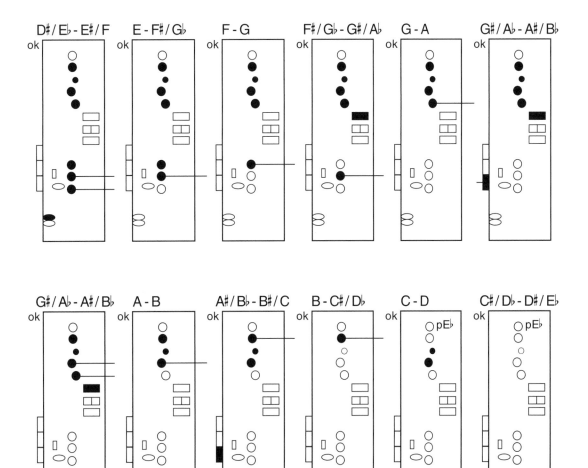

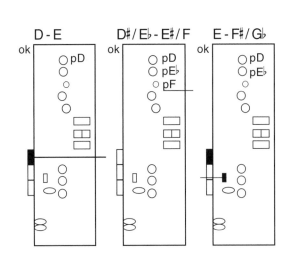

Fig. 4.6. Whole-Step Trills

TRILL EXERCISES FOR TECHNIQUE DEVELOPMENT

An excellent exercise for developing independent finger speed and dexterity is based on the whole step and half step trill fingering charts.

To gain maximum benefits from this exercise:

- Use a metronome.
- Start about quarter note = 60 and increase the speed gradually.
- Maintain good hand position.
- Move the fingers quickly with a "snap."

Practice any major or minor scale in one octave. Every key presents different finger coordination challenges. As always, maintain a good tone. To exercise the finger motion fully, lift the fingers high but still retain correct hand position.

Use the following rhythm examples for all intervals.

Exercise 4.1. Trill Practice 1

Fig. 4.7. Trill Exercise 1

Exercise 4.2. Trill Practice 2

Fig. 4.8. Trill Exercise 2

Exercise 4.3. Trill Practice 3

Fig. 4.9. Trill Exercise 3

LOW AND HIGH REGISTERS

There are two common weaknesses among most saxophonists: poor technique in the high register (palm keys) and in the low register (spatula keys). The primary reason is that saxophonists spend much less time in those registers—avoiding them, in fact. As the music becomes more advanced and places greater demands on technique in the high and low registers, saxophonists discover this glaring flaw in their technical facility. It is easy to practice strengths and avoid weaknesses. However, to truly gain mastery of the high and low registers, they must be directly addressed. The low and high register studies take little time in a practice session but will produce amazing results. An added benefit is that subdivision skills improve as well. Spend just a few minutes a day on the low and high register studies, and see how quickly your technique improves.

LOW REGISTER STUDY

The examples are shown in C major. Add accidentals to transpose them to other keys. For example, for the key of G major, add one sharp; key of D major, add two sharps, etc.

Exercise 4.4. Low Register Practice 1

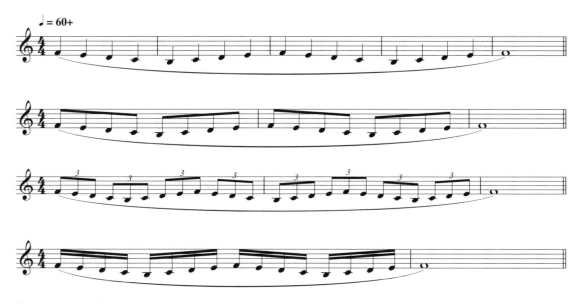

Fig. 4.10. Low Register 1

Exercise 4.5. Low Register Practice 2

Fig. 4.11. Low Register 2

HIGH REGISTER STUDY

The examples are shown in C major. Add accidentals to transpose them to other keys. For example, for the key of F major, add one flat. For the key of B♭ major, add two flats, etc.

Exercise 4.6. High Register Exercise 1

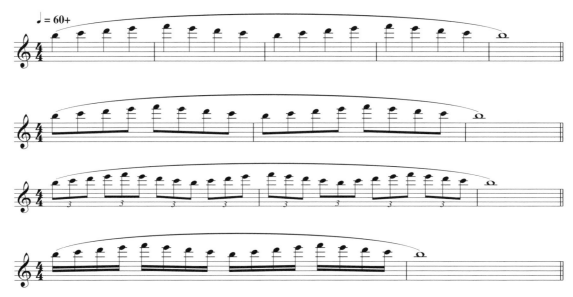

Fig. 4.12. High Register 1

Exercise 4.7. High Register Exercise 2

Fig. 4.13. High Register 2

ARTICULATION

"Attack" and "release" are common articulation terms. Whatever terminology is used, how to begin and end a musical pitch is a skill that must be learned early. The saxophonist must be able to perform articulations ranging from legato to spiccato.

When your embouchure is secure and controlled, it is time to acquire proper articulation. For the overwhelming majority of saxophonists, the "tip to tip" style of articulation should be used. The tip of the tongue touches approximately 1/16 inch below the reed tip, producing a light, delicate attack. Contacting the reed further away from the reed tip produces progressively heavier articulations. An alternate method, anchor tonguing, works for a few who have longer tongues. The tip is anchored at the base of the bottom front row teeth, and the middle portion of the tongue makes contact with the reed. How long is long? If you can touch the bottom of your jaw with your tongue, it's long.

Tune the saxophone to A440. Then, using just the neck and mouthpiece, produce a steady pitch. Start the air slowly, and then increase the velocity. After many successful repetitions using the neck only, try to reproduce the same articulation with the entire saxophone. Step by step, the articulation process is as follows:

1. Form the embouchure.
2. Drop the jaw slightly, and take a breath through the mouth.
3. Touch the tip of the reed with the tip of the tongue.
4. Build air pressure in the oral cavity, and gently remove the tongue from the reed.
   - Air pressure starts the tone.
   - Remember to stop the tone by "tapering," as described on page 39.

Legato

The first articulation that should be learned is legato. Legato connects notes rather than separates them, as in staccato. Practice legato at first with the neck and mouthpiece, as mentioned previously. Maintain a continuous airflow similar to slurring. When the tongue makes contact with the reed, the reed's vibrations are stopped, which produces the desired articulation. Air pressure and muscular support are continuous. Contact the reed about a sixteenth of an inch from the tip as though "brushing" the reed with the tongue.

Staccato

There are two basic methods of staccato: air release and tongue release. The choice is based on note duration and tempo. Slower tempo staccato notes are air released, and rapid staccato notes are tongue released. To produce a short air-released staccato note, use a single "puff" of air produced by a quick thrust of the abdominal muscles, similar to a silent cough.

At faster tempos, it becomes physically impossible to play staccato notes short enough when releasing by air. Air and tongue releases eventually merge to where the end of one articulation becomes the beginning of the next: rapid staccato. If in doubt whether to choose air or tongue release, try both. Which sounds the most musical?

PRACTICE

The three basic articulations (involving tongue action) are legato, breath release staccato, and tongue release staccato. All others such as marcato, accent, sforzando, etc. are derivatives of these. To develop consistent and precise legato and staccato articulations, practice the two exercises on the next page until they are second nature. All bpm markings are approximate, depending on the proficiency level of the saxophonist.

Exercise 4.8. Legato

Pick any note in the middle register such as third space C or third line B. To maintain good tone and note connection, keep the airflow steady. The tip of the tongue should be forward and close to the reed tip. Use a light, brushing action (see page 74). Practice several articulations at each bpm marking until you can go smoothly from 60 to approximately 200 with each articulation receiving the same emphasis. Gradually move into the upper, then lower registers

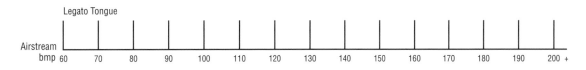

Fig. 4.14. Legato Exercise

Exercise 4.9. Breath Release Staccato to Tongue Release Staccato

Again, pick a note in the middle register. Play steady notes 60 bpm to 180 bpm using a breath-release staccato. Be sure to taper each note (see page 39). From about 180 bpm and higher, use a tongue-release staccato. Practice a series of articulations at each individual tempo. After some time, see if you can gradually go from 60 bpm to 200+ bmp without a metronome, making the transition from breath release to tongue release so subtle that a listener cannot identify when it occurs.

Fig. 4.15. Staccato Exercise

CHAPTER 5

Practice and Preparation

"Observe everything. Communicate well."
—Frank Thomas, Disney Animator

CONTEMPORARY REPERTOIRE

In the 1970s, a rapid increase in the number of new compositions for saxophone included new contemporary techniques, also designated as *extended techniques*. The formation of the World Saxophone Congress, in 1969, prompted composers to seek new ways of expression in their compositions. Future Saxophone Congress meetings would be forthcoming all over the world, and there would be many more premiers. There is a great deal of merit to pursuing these contemporary compositions. A performer is "stretched," and will discover new capabilities of the saxophone and personal performance skills previously thought impossible. Learning these techniques requires resourcefulness and patience. Prerecorded accompaniments challenge a performer's concept of time and space.

I discovered a sequence of four compositions, chosen from among many, that systematically introduces these techniques to students who are intrigued enough to pursue them.

"Improvisation I" by Ryo Noda

The first suggested composition is "Improvisation I" (c. 4 minutes) by Japanese saxophonist Ryo Noda. It is unaccompanied and includes the following extended techniques:

- vibrato manipulation
- quarter steps sharp and flat
- Japanese cutting tone
- flutter tonguing
- portamento
- resonance fingerings
- rhythmic improvisation

There is a page of explanation along with the written symbols for these effects, provided by Noda. Recordings are also available for study.

"Sketch for Alto Saxophone" by Ronald Caravan

The second composition is "Sketch for Alto Saxophone" (c. 4 minutes) by saxophonist Ronald Caravan. It contains some of the same techniques as in "Improvisation I" but introduces several more:

- timbre variation with fingerings
- multiphonics
- key slaps
- resonance trills
- reverse envelope
- three quarter-steps sharp and flat
- dark/bright tone quality
- smorzato
- rolling tone

"Sketch" is unaccompanied, allowing some flexibility for timed entrances. An explanatory page of the extended technique symbols is included.

A Selection with a Prerecorded Accompaniment

The third selection can be any of the numerous compositions published that include tape/CD/DVD, etc. Since these compositions are with prerecorded media, the performer takes on an additional challenge: timing. The primary extended technique learned is matching saxophone notation to media notation in a timing sequence.

"Squirt for Alto Saxophone, Live Electronics, and Tape" by Pete Stollery

The fourth composition is the ultimate challenge. "Squirt for Alto Saxophone, Live Electronics, and Tape" is by Pete Stollery at Aberdeen University in Scotland (11 minutes, currently unpublished but available through the composer). Composed for and premiered by Douglas Skinner, this complex piece requires the saxophonist to use three microphones (keys, bell, voice), in addition to the saxophone itself. It is an intricate and difficult work, demanding a performer to use all his/her resources. In addition to the extended techniques already mentioned, "Squirt..." adds:

- long, smooth glissandos
- senza misura
- alternative fingerings above noteheads
- air tone (breath only)
- key slaps
- slap tonguing
- a stopwatch
- vocal sounds into a microphone

Additional Repertoire

There are many other compositions that include extended techniques that can be substituted. To understand and learn to perform this type of music is a formidable task. The task is simplified if it can be done in stages, small steps at a time. When practicing such a composition the following suggestions might be helpful:

- Allow plenty of time for rehearsal before a performance.
- The amount of detail in the composer's legend helps.
- Correspond with the composer, if possible.
- Learn the piece "inch by inch."
- Use a magnifying glass on the music to avoid skipping small details.
- Preplan the practice session—the amount of music to learn.
- Learn episodes unaccompanied at first.
- Practice new material, then repeat the entire piece to that point from the beginning.
- Match media sounds on the saxophone, if that is the composer's intention.
- Listen extensively to the recording with a stopwatch for timing (no instrument).
- Practice with stopwatch for approximate timings.
- Then practice with tape and stopwatch for correct timing.

CREATIVE PRACTICE

When a saxophonist enters a practice room, it is a crucial moment. The next hour or so can be rewarding with much accomplished, or it can be a complete waste of time. A successful practice session is dependent on many factors. Frame of mind, specific goals, organization of time, and a predetermined routine all directly affect the outcome of a practice session. Practicing correct fundamentals and employing creative practice methods are more important than the length of the session.

Beginning saxophonists are somewhat limited in their musical scope. Their primary focus is on notes and rests, rhythm, and basic articulation. More advanced players are often guilty of mindless practice where they also can be limited to the musical basics. Every attempt must be made to pay attention to the finer details of the music when in the practice room. Less advanced players spend most of their time in the left column on the chart on the following page. Ideally, spend as much time as possible in the right column.

—————————————————→

notes and rests	dynamics
rhythm	flexible tempos
basic articulation	timbre change/tone color
	vibrato speed
	airflow
	form and analysis
	articulation subtleties
	execution of ornaments
	style and interpretation
	etc.

Here is a "Lesson Assignment Form" that can be used by teachers or by students who want to organize their practice sessions. This form provides structure for both the lesson and practice room sessions.

Saxophone Studio Lesson Assignment

Name _____

Date _____

Warm-Ups _____

_____

_____

_____

_____

Etudes _____

_____

Literature _____

_____

Jazz _____

_____

CD _____

_____

Comments _____

_____

_____

_____

_____

Fig. 5.1. Lesson Assignment Form

The "Lesson Assignment Form" can be altered to suit your particular needs. A student should take the form to the practice room, either completed by the teacher or completed himself/herself before a practice session. Allot a specified amount of time to all phases, from warm-ups to playing along with a recording or listening to it. Include sight-reading, as well. Over a period of a few months, the versatility and value of the "Lesson Assignment Form" will become evident.

PRACTICE ROOM TIPS

Learning to practice creatively requires effective technical and musical tactics. Some proven suggestions are listed below:

Technique Drills:

1. Play slowly and accurately along with an electronic metronome. Gradually increase the tempo 2 or 3 beats per minute until the final tempo is reached.

2. Isolate one beat, and repeat it ten to twenty times. Move to the next beat, then the next beat, etc.

3. Place a fermata over an important note in a technical passage. This allows the fingers to temporarily relax and allows the eye to look ahead.

4. Repeat notes in groups of twos (C D, C D, E F, E F, etc.).

5. Practice dotted rhythms.

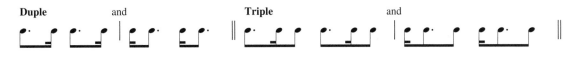

Fig. 5.2. Practice Rhythms

Playing with Expression:

1. Place breath marks in the music with a pencil, both primary and secondary.

2. Make notations of fingerings, crescendos, decrescendos, and dynamic markings.

3. Conduct the music while singing the melody.

4. Rely on subdivision to play accurate rhythms.

5. Match the speed of vibrato to the degree of intensity in the musical line.

6. Know where a phrase begins and ends.

7. Identify the climactic note(s) in a phrase.

8. Create tension and release as the phrase dictates.

PRESENTING A RECITAL

Presenting a first solo or ensemble public performance is an enormous undertaking and a valuable learning experience. It is considerably easier the second time. Hours and hours of focused practice are required to prepare the music, organize details, and promote it. Every performer has experienced the sudden pressure of realizing an important detail was forgotten and the ensuing panic that follows. It is an excellent idea to keep a Recital Checklist. Each finished step receives a check mark. By systematically taking care of business, the recital will be more enjoyable for both the performer and the audience.

Recital Checklist

Three to four months before the recital:

☐ select music
☐ contact other performers
☐ start practicing
☐ reserve the hall

Two months before the recital:

☐ obtain commitments from other performers
☐ practice harder

One month before the recital:

☐ select dress rehearsal date(s) with other performers/accompanist
☐ begin rehearsals

Two weeks before the recital:

☐ check on recording engineer
☐ arrange for special parking, if needed
☐ get page turner for accompanist
☐ get stage crew for moving of stands, equipment, etc.
☐ proof the program
☐ submit program for printing, along with program notes
☐ send invitations to friends, family; notify newspapers and do publicity posters
☐ check scheduling of piano tuner
☐ arrange for special details such as sound system, any lighting effects, accessory equipment, reception room, food and drink, anything to be used before, during, and after performance
☐ remind everybody, discuss concert attire

A few days before the recital:

☐ pick up programs
☐ have dress rehearsal
☐ remind everybody of the details again
☐ review this entire checklist to make sure nothing was overlooked

After all of this, go have a great performance!

JAZZ STYLE BASICS

The key to teaching or learning basic jazz styles begins with articulations and swing eighth notes. Jazz arrangements look one way on paper but sound another when performed. Printed notes are merely representations of a desired style, and it is up to the performer to interpret them to fit the style of the arrangement.

Three articulation markings are commonly found in jazz arrangements:

> \>   tongue accent, note is full value
> \^   heavy accent, starting and stopping the note with the tongue; sometimes, though, it is used as a type of staccato
> −   no accent, full value, legato tongue

The triplet subdivision, with occasional accents on the third note of the triplet, is fundamental to the swing eighth-note "feel." Even experienced jazz students often play the dotted eighth/sixteenth version without realizing it.

Fig. 5.3. Swing Feel, not Straight Feel

Jazz arrangers typically just write straight eighth notes, but they are intended to be interpreted with a swing feel.

Fig. 5.4. Written Eighth Notes

To play in the swing eighth-note style:

a. Play the passage slowly, articulating all notes of the triplet.

b. Tie the first two triplet notes together, maintaining all notes at full value.

c. Accent the third note of the triplet.

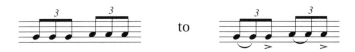

Fig. 5.5. "Swing" Feel

Achieving saxophone excellence is a lifelong learning process. There is much to learn and apply to your pursuit. Hopefully, the information in *The Saxophone Handbook: A Complete Guide to Tone, Technique, Maintenance, and Performance* will make the journey more interesting and productive.

Resources

The following references provide additional information.

SAXOPHONE PEDAGOGY

Pedagogy sources contain information on many aspects of teaching and playing the saxophone such as psychology, interpretation, phrasing, technique, rhythm, acoustics, breathing, and much more. Some of the sources are clarinet and flute texts that are particularly informative regarding phrasing and interpretation.

Galway, James. *Flute*. New York: Schirmer Books, 1982.

Green, Barry and Timothy Gallowey. *The Inner Game of Music*. Garden City: Anchor Press, 1986.

Kirck, George T. *The Reed Guide*. Chicago: Reed-Mate Co., 1983.

Krell, John. *Kincaidiana*. Culver City: Trio Associates, 1973.

Liebman, David. *Developing a Personal Saxophone Sound*. Medfield: Dorn Publications Inc., 1989.

Mauk, Steven. *A Practical Approach to Playing the Saxophone*. Ithaca, New York: Steven Mauk, 1984.

Opperman, Kalmen. *Handbook for Making and Adjusting Single Reeds*. New York: Chappell & Co., 1956.

Pino, David. *The Clarinet and Clarinet Playing*. New York: Charles Scribner's & Sons, 1980.

Stein, Keith. *The Art of Clarinet Playing*. Evanston: Summy-Birchard Company, 1958.

Teal, Larry. *The Art of Saxophone Playing*. Evanston: Summy-Birchard Inc., 1963.

Teal, Larry. *The Saxophonist's Manual*. Ann Arbor: Encore, 1978.

Thurmond, James Morgan. *Note Grouping*. Detroit: Harlo Press, 1982.

SAXOPHONE REPAIR

Goodson, Steve. *The Steve Goodson Saxophone Repair Video.* MusicMedic.com.

Saska, Ronald. *Guide to Repairing Woodwinds.* Glenmoore: Roncorp Publications, 1987.

Singer, Bill. *Saxophone Repair Made Easy.* Videos, Vol. I–III, New York: SingerLand Productions Inc., 1993.

OVERTONES AND ALTISSIMO

Allard, Joe. *Three Octave Scales and Chords.* New York: Charles Colin, 1979.

Lang, Rosemary. *Beginning Studies in the Altissimo Register.* Indianapolis: Lang Music Publications, 1971.

Luckey, Robert A. *Saxophone Altissimo: High Note Development for the Contemporary Player.* Lafayette: Olympia Music Publishing, 1992.

Nash, Ted. *Studies in High Harmonics for the Tenor and Alto Saxophones.* New York: MCA Music, 1946.

Rascher, Sigurd. *Top Tones for the Saxophone.* New York: Carl Fischer Inc., 1977.

Rousseau, Eugene. *Saxophone High Tones, A Systematic Approach to the Above-Normal Range of the Saxophones: Soprano, Alto, Tenor, Baritone.* Shell Lake: Etoile Music Inc., 1978.

Sinta, Donald J. and Denise C. Dabney. *"Voicing:" An Approach to the Saxophone's Third Register.* Laurel: Sintafest Music Company, 1992.

Teal, Larry. *The Art of Saxophone Playing.* Princeton: Summy-Birchard Inc., 1963.

SAXOPHONE HISTORY

Baines, Anthony. *Woodwind Instruments and Their History.* New York: W. W. Norton and Company Inc., 1957.

Gee, Harry. *Saxophone Soloists and Their Music: 1844-1985.* Bloomington: Indiana University Press, 1986.

Horwood, Wally. *Adolphe Sax 1814-1894: His Life and Legacy.* Baldock, Herts: Egon Publishers Ltd., 1983.

Kochnitzkey, Leon. *Adolphe Sax and His Saxophone.* Chicago: World Saxophone Congress, 1972.

Kool, Jaap. *Das Saxophon.* Baldock, Hertfordshire: Egon Publishers, 1987.

About the Author

Douglas Skinner is professor emeritus at Texas State University. Mr. Skinner taught saxophone, band instrument repair, jazz ensemble, jazz/rock history, and woodwind methods for over forty years. He holds bachelor of music and master of music education degrees from the University of North Texas. As a concert soloist, Mr. Skinner has performed in the United States, England, Poland, Scotland, Russia, Turkey, and Mexico. He was also soprano saxophonist in the Nova Saxophone Quartet. The quartet's recordings *InNOVAtions, Double Image*, and *Outside the Box* were released on the Musical Heritage Society and Equilibrium labels. Mr. Skinner's publications include articles in *Jazz Educators Journal, Saxophone Symposium*, and *Popular Musicians*. In addition, he has authored twenty-seven essays in various encyclopedias. Mr. Skinner served four terms as interim director of the School of Music at Texas State University.

INDEX

Note: Page numbers in *italics* indicate illustrations or figures.